Microsoft® Office Excel® 2007

Level 3 (Second Edition)

Microsoft® Office Excel® 2007: Level 3 (Second Edition)

Part Number: 084892
Course Edition: 1.10

NOTICES

What is the Microsoft Business Certification Program?

The Microsoft Business Certification Program enables candidates to show that they have something exceptional to offer – proven expertise in Microsoft Office programs. The two certification tracks allow candidates to choose how they want to exhibit their skills, either through validating skills within a specific Microsoft product or taking their knowledge to the next level and combining Microsoft programs to show that they can apply multiple skill sets to complete more complex office tasks. Recognized by businesses and schools around the world, over 3 million certifications have been obtained in over 100 different countries. The Microsoft Business Certification Program is the only Microsoft-approved certification program of its kind.

What is the Microsoft Certified Application Specialist Certification?

HELP US IMPROVE OUR COURSEWARE

Your comments are important to us. Please contact us at Element K Press LLC, 1-800-478-7788, 500 Canal View Boulevard, Rochester, NY 14623, Attention: Product Planning, or through our Web site at **http://support.elementkcourseware.com**.

The Microsoft Certified Application Specialist Certification exams focus on validating specific skill sets within each of the Microsoft® Office system programs. The candidate can choose which exam(s) they want to take according to which skills they want to validate. The available Application Specialist exams include:

- Using Microsoft®Windows Vista™
- Using Microsoft® Office Word 2007
- Using Microsoft® Office Excel® 2007
- Using Microsoft® Office PowerPoint® 2007
- Using Microsoft® Office Access 2007
- Using Microsoft® Office Outlook® 2007

What is the Microsoft Certified Application Professional Certification?

The Microsoft Certified Application Professional Certification exams focus on a candidate's ability to use the 2007 Microsoft® Office system to accomplish industry-agnostic functions, for example Budget Analysis and Forecasting, or Content Management and Collaboration. The available Application Professional exams currently include:

- Organizational Support
- Creating and Managing Presentations
- Content Management and Collaboration
- Budget Analysis and Forecasting

What do the Microsoft Business Certification Vendor of Approved Courseware logos represent?

The logos validate that the courseware has been approved by the Microsoft® Business Certification Vendor program and that these courses cover objectives that will be included in the relevant exam. It also means that after utilizing this courseware, you may be prepared to pass the exams required to become a Microsoft Certified Application Specialist or Microsoft Certified Application Professional.

For more information:

To learn more about Microsoft Certified Application Specialist or Professional exams, visit **www.microsoft.com/learning/msbc**.

To learn about other Microsoft Certified Application Specialist approved courseware from Element K, visit **www.elementkcourseware.com**.

∗ The availability of Microsoft Certified Application exams varies by Microsoft Office program, program version and language. Visit **www.microsoft.com/learning** for exam availability.

Microsoft, the Office Logo, Outlook, and PowerPoint are either registered trademarks or trademarks of Microsoft Corporation in the United States and/or other countries. The Microsoft Certified Application Specialist and Microsoft Certified Application Professional Logos are used under license from Microsoft Corporation.

Microsoft® Office Excel® 2007: Level 3 (Second Edition)

About This Course

Your training in and use of Microsoft® Office Excel® 2007 has provided you with a solid foundation in the basic and intermediate skills for working in Excel. You have used Excel to perform tasks such as running calculations on data and sorting and filtering numeric data. In this course, you will extend your knowledge into some of the more specialized and advanced capabilities of Excel by automating some common tasks, applying advanced analysis techniques to more complex data sets, collaborating on worksheets with others, and sharing Excel data with other applications.

Advanced analysis techniques help you extract more value from your static data by summarizing and forecasting values that are not readily apparent. Using collaboration techniques helps you add value to your data and analysis of the data by allowing you to incorporate the feedback of others into your data.

This course can also benefit you if you are preparing to take the Microsoft Certified Application Specialist exam for Microsoft® Excel® 2007. Please refer to the CD-ROM that came with this course for a document that maps exam objectives to the content in the Microsoft Office Excel Courseware series. To access the mapping document, insert the CD-ROM into your CD-ROM drive and at the root of the ROM, double-click ExamMapping.doc to open the mapping document. In addition to the mapping document, two assessment files per course can be found on the CD-ROM to check your knowledge. To access the assessments, at the root of the course part number folder, double-click 084892s3.doc to view the assessments without the answers marked, or double-click 084892ie.doc to view the assessments with the answers marked.

Course Description

Target Student

This course was designed for students desiring to gain the skills necessary to create macros, collaborate with others, audit and analyze worksheet data, incorporate multiple data sources, and import and export data. In addition, the course is also for students desiring to prepare for the Microsoft Certified Application Specialist exam in Microsoft® Office Excel® 2007, and who already have knowledge of the basics of Excel, including how to create, edit, format, and print worksheets that include charts and sorted and filtered data.

Course Prerequisites

To ensure your success, we recommend you first take the following Element K courses or have equivalent knowledge:

- Microsoft® Office Excel® 2007 Level 1
- Microsoft® Office Excel® 2007 Level 2

How to Use This Book

As a Learning Guide

Each lesson covers one broad topic or set of related topics. Lessons are arranged in order of increasing proficiency with *Microsoft® Office Excel® 2007*; skills you acquire in one lesson are used and developed in subsequent lessons. For this reason, you should work through the lessons in sequence.

We organized each lesson into results-oriented topics. Topics include all the relevant and supporting information you need to master *Excel 2007*, and activities allow you to apply this information to practical hands-on examples.

You get to try out each new skill on a specially prepared sample file. This saves you typing time and allows you to concentrate on the skill at hand. Through the use of sample files, hands-on activities, illustrations that give you feedback at crucial steps, and supporting background information, this book provides you with the foundation and structure to learn *Excel 2007* quickly and easily.

As a Review Tool

Any method of instruction is only as effective as the time and effort you are willing to invest in it. In addition, some of the information that you learn in class may not be important to you immediately, but it may become important later on. For this reason, we encourage you to spend some time reviewing the topics and activities after the course. For additional challenge when reviewing activities, try the "What You Do" column before looking at the "How You Do It" column.

As a Reference

The organization and layout of the book make it easy to use as a learning tool and as an after-class reference. You can use this book as a first source for definitions of terms, background information on given topics, and summaries of procedures.

Course Icons

Icon	Description
	A **Caution Note** makes students aware of potential negative consequences of an action, setting, or decision that are not easily known.
	Display Slide provides a prompt to the instructor to display a specific slide. Display Slides are included in the Instructor Guide only.
	An **Instructor Note** is a comment to the instructor regarding delivery, classroom strategy, classroom tools, exceptions, and other special considerations. Instructor Notes are included in the Instructor Guide only.
	Notes Page indicates a page that has been left intentionally blank for students to write on.
	A **Student Note** provides additional information, guidance, or hints about a topic or task.
	A **Version Note** indicates information necessary for a specific version of software.

Certification

This course is designed to help you prepare for the following certification.

Certification Path: Microsoft Certified Application Specialist – Excel® 2007

This course is one of a series of Element K courseware titles that addresses Microsoft Certified Application Specialist (Microsoft Business Certification) skill sets. The Microsoft Certified Application Specialist program is for individuals who use Microsoft's business desktop software and who seek recognition for their expertise with specific Microsoft products. Certification candidates must pass one or more proficiency exams in order to earn Microsoft Certified Application Specialist certification.

Course Objectives

In this course, you will automate some common Excel tasks, apply advanced analysis techniques to more complex data sets, collaborate on worksheets with others, and share Excel data with other applications.

You will:

- increase productivity and improve efficiency by streamlining your workflow.
- collaborate with others using workbooks.
- audit worksheets.
- analyze data.
- work with multiple workbooks.
- import and export data.
- use Excel with the web.
- structure workbooks with XML.

Course Requirements

Hardware

Hardware Requirements for Classroom Computers

For this course, you will need one computer for each student and one for the instructor. Each computer will need the following minimum hardware components:

- A 1 GHz Pentium-class processor or faster.
- A minimum of 256 MB of RAM. 512 MB of RAM is recommended.
- A 10 GB hard disk or larger. You should have at least 1 GB of free hard disk space available for the Office installation.
- A CD-ROM drive.
- A keyboard and mouse or other pointing device.
- A 1024 x 768 resolution monitor is recommended.
- Network cards and cabling for local network access.
- Internet access (contact your local network administrator).
- A projection system to display the instructor's computer screen.

Software

- Microsoft Office Professional Edition 2007
- Microsoft Office Suite Service Pack 1
- Windows XP Professional with Service Pack 2

  This course was developed using the Windows XP operating system; however, the manufacturer's documentation states that it will also run on Vista. If you use Vista, you might notice some slight differences when keying the course.

Class Setup

For Initial Class Setup

1. Install Windows XP Professional with SP2 on an empty partition.

   - Leave the Administrator password blank.

   - For all other installation parameters, use values that are appropriate for your environment (see your local network administrator for details).

2. On Windows XP Professional, disable the Welcome screen. (This step ensures that students will be able to log on as the Administrator user regardless of what other user accounts exist on the computer.)

   a. Click Start and choose Control Panel→User Accounts.

   b. Click Change The Way Users Log On And Off.

   c. Uncheck Use Welcome Screen.

   d. Click Apply Options.

3. On Windows XP Professional, install Service Pack 2. Use the Service Pack installation defaults.

4. Run the Internet Connection Wizard to set up the Internet connection as appropriate for your environment, if you did not do so during installation.

5. Display known file type extensions.

   a. Open Windows Explorer (right-click Start and then select Explore).

   b. Choose Tools→Folder Options.

   c. On the View tab, in the Advanced Settings list box, uncheck Hide Extensions For Known File Types.

   d. Click Apply, and then click OK.

   e. Close Windows Explorer.

6. Log on to the computer as the Administrator user if you have not already done so.

7. Perform a Complete installation of Microsoft Office Professional 2007.

8. In the User Name dialog box, click OK to accept the default user name and initials.

9. In the Microsoft Office 2007 Activation Wizard dialog box, click Next to activate the Office 2007 application.

10. When the activation of Microsoft Office 2007 is complete, click Close to close the Microsoft Office 2007 Activation Wizard dialog box.

11. In the User Name dialog box, click OK.

12. In the Welcome To Microsoft 2007! dialog box, click Finish. You must have an active Internet connection in order to complete this step. Here, you select the Download And Install Updates From Microsoft Update When Available (Recommended) option, so that whenever there is a new update, it gets automatically installed in your system.

13. After the Microsoft Update runs, in the Microsoft Office dialog box, click OK.

14. Minimize the Language Bar, if necessary.

15. On the course CD-ROM, open the 084_892 folder. Then, open the Data folder. Run the 084892dd.exe self-extracting file located within. This will install a folder named 084892Data on your C drive. This folder contains all the data files that you will use to complete this course.

Within each lesson folder, you may find a Solution folder. This folder contains solution files for the lesson's activities and lesson lab, which can be used by students to check their end results.

Create a Digital Certificate on Every Computer

Perform this setup procedure on every computer.

1. Choose Start→All Programs→Microsoft Office→Microsoft Office Tools→Digital Certificate for VBA Projects.

2. In the Create Digital Certificate dialog box, in the Your Certificate's Name text box, type a unique name for the certificate, and click OK.

It is recommended that you use a generic name such as Student01 on the first computer. Then, on the second computer, repeat this step and name the certificate Student02. Continue in this manner until each computer has one uniquely named digital certificate.

3. Click OK to close the success message box.

Before Every Class

1. Log on to the computer as the Administrator user.

2. Delete any existing data files from the C:\084892Data folder.

3. Extract a fresh copy of the course data files from the CD-ROM provided with the course manual.

List of Additional Files

Printed with each activity is a list of files students open to complete that activity. Many activities also require additional files that students do not open, but are needed to support the file(s) students are working with. These supporting files are included with the student data files on the course CD-ROM or data disk. Do not delete these files.

1 | Streamlining Workflow

Lesson Time: 1 hour(s), 10 minutes

Lesson Objectives:

In this lesson, you will increase productivity and improve efficiency by streamlining your workflow.

You will:

- Create a macro.
- Edit a macro.
- Apply conditional formatting.
- Add data validation criteria.
- Update a workbook's properties.
- Modify Excel's default settings.

Introduction

You have identified common tasks you repeat in Microsoft® Office Excel® 2007. You would now like to simplify the methods you use to complete these tasks. In this lesson, you will streamline your workflow.

While working with workbooks in Excel, there may be times when you need to automate frequently performed tasks, restrict the type of data entered in the cells, or format data based on predefined criteria. Streamlining your workflow by tailoring the Excel environment to your job needs can increase your productivity and improve your efficiency.

TOPIC A
Create a Macro

You have used Excel enough to know that there are certain tasks you repeat. You now need a way to automate repeated tasks so they can be performed with minimal interaction by you. In this topic, you will create a macro.

You are developing a workbook that contains 20 worksheets. Cells A1 through D1 of every worksheet contain your name, your company's name, your division in the company, and your manager's name, respectively. Would you like to type that data into each cell on each worksheet? Wouldn't it be easier to type the data once on the first worksheet and then add the data to each of the remaining worksheets just by clicking a button? Macros automate complex tasks and ensure their precise replication.

Macros

Definition:

A *macro* is a task automation tool that executes a set of commands to automate frequently repeated steps. Each macro is uniquely identified by a macro name. A macro-enabled Excel Workbook has .xlsm as the file extension. You can use the macro recorder to record a sequence of actions, and then perform these tasks by using the macro name or a simple command assigned to the macro. The set of commands in the recorded macro is converted into programming code that can be edited if required. A macro can be stored in workbooks or templates. If a macro is stored in a template, you can test it in any new document you create based on the template.

Example:

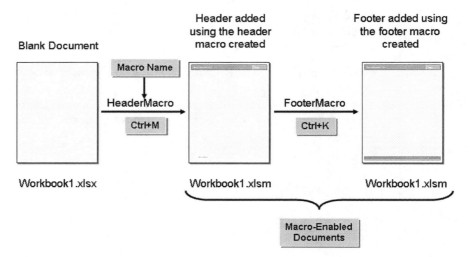

The Record Macro Dialog Box

The Record Macro dialog box is used to specify details about a macro and to start recording the macro. You can specify details such as the macro name, shortcut key, location in which the macro will be stored, and description of the macro in the Record Macro dialog box.

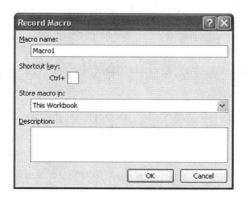

Figure 1-1: *The Record Macro dialog box with options for beginning and setting the recording options for a macro.*

Macro Naming Rules

There are certain rules to follow when you create macro names:

- The name must begin with a letter.
- The name must not contain spaces.
- The name can contain letters, numbers, and the underscore character.

If any of these rules are not followed, you will receive an invalid procedure name error message.

How to Create a Macro

Procedure Reference: Create a Macro

To create a macro:

1. Select the worksheet where you want to begin recording the macro.
2. On the View tab, in the Macros group, click the Macros button drop-down arrow and select Record Macro to open the Record Macro dialog box.
3. In the Record Macro dialog box, in the Macro Name text box, type a name for the macro.
4. In the Shortcut Key text box, type a letter to add a shortcut key for the macro.

 Ctrl appears by default when you open the Record Macro dialog box to specify the shortcut key. This combination is a quick way to run a macro in a worksheet.

5. From the Store Macro In drop-down list, select the location where the macro will be saved.
6. In the Description text box, add a description of the macro.
7. Click OK to begin recording the macro.

8. Perform the tasks you want to record in the macro.

9. Stop the recording.

   - Click the Stop Recording button on the Microsoft Office Status Bar.
   - Or, on the View tab, in the Macros group, click the Macros button drop-down arrow, and select Stop Recording.

10. From the File menu, choose Save As, and from the Save As drop-down list, select the .xlsm file extension to save the macro along with the workbook.

Procedure Reference: Run Macros Using the Macros Dialog Box

To run macros using the Macros dialog box:

1. Choose the worksheet to which you want to apply the macro.

2. On the View tab, in the Macros group, from the Macros drop-down list, select View Macros.

3. In the Macro dialog box, in the macro list box, select the macro you want to apply.

4. Click Run.

ACTIVITY 1-1

Creating a Macro

Data Files:

Office Supplies.xlsx

Before You Begin:

From the C:\084892Data\Streamlining Workflow folder, open Office Supplies.xlsx.

Scenario:

You are developing a file that tracks the expenditures on office supplies. The file contains five worksheets, and you want to apply the same formatting to four of them.

You want to make the following changes to the Australian, European, North American, and Summary sheets:

● Change the font color and font size of the cell that contains each worksheet's title to light green and 24 points, respectively.

● Bold and italicize the column headings.

● Format the numerical data to currency.

Rather than making the changes to all four sheets manually, you have decided to format one of the sheets, record the actions, and automate the actions on the remaining sheets by using a shortcut.

What You Do	How You Do It
1. **Begin recording a new macro in the Office Supplies workbook.**	a. In Office Supplies.xlsx, **select the Australian worksheet tab.**
	b. On the View tab, in the Macros group, **click the Macros button drop-down arrow, and select Record Macro.**
	c. In the Record Macro dialog box, in the Macro Name text box, **type *SheetFormat***
	d. Observe that Ctrl appears by default before the Shortcut Key text box and, in the text box, **type *m***
	e. In the Description text box, **type *Worksheet Formats***
	f. **Click OK** to begin recording the macro.

2.	Make changes to the font size and color of the Australian worksheet's title.	a. **Click cell A1.**
		b. On the Home tab, in the Font group, from the Font Size drop-down list, **select 24.**
		c. From the Font Color drop-down list, in the Standard Colors section, **select the fifth color from the left** to display the title in light green.
3.	Add bold and italic formats to the column headings.	a. **Select the range of cells from A3 through E3.**
		b. In the Font group, **click the Bold button.**
		c. **Click the Italic button.**
4.	Apply currency formatting to the numerical data.	a. **Select the range of cells from B4 through E9.**
		b. In the Number group, from the Number Format drop-down list, **select Currency.**
5.	Stop recording the macro.	a. On the Ribbon, **select the View tab.**
		b. In the Macros group, **click the Macros button drop-down arrow, and select Stop Recording.**
6.	Run the macro on the European worksheet.	a. **Select the European worksheet tab.**
		b. **Click the Macros button drop-down arrow and select View Macros.**
		c. In the Macro dialog box, observe that the SheetFormat macro is selected and **click Run.**
		d. Observe that the macro has been used to format the sheet.

	A	B	C	D	E
1	European Division				
2					
3	*Item*	*QTR 1*	*QTR 2*	*QTR 3*	*QTR 4*
4	Hardware	$ 400.00	$ 800.00	$ 900.00	$ 300.00
5	Software	$ 200.00	$ 500.00	$1,200.00	$ 100.00
6	Furniture	$ 300.00	$ 400.00	$1,400.00	$ 300.00
7	Accessories	$ 100.00	$ 300.00	$ 500.00	$ 300.00
8					
9	*Totals:*	$1,000.00	$2,000.00	$4,000.00	$1,000.00
10					

7. **Apply the macro to the North American and Summary worksheets using the keyboard shortcut.**

   a. **Select the North American worksheet tab and press Ctrl+M** to apply the macro using the keyboard shortcut.

   b. **Select the Summary worksheet tab and press Ctrl+M.**

   c. In the File Name text box, **type *My Office Supplies***

   d. From the Save As Type drop-down list, **select Excel Macro-Enabled Workbook (*.xlsm).**

   e. **Click Save.**

TOPIC B
Edit a Macro

You have created macros in Excel. You now need to change a macro you have already created. In this topic, you will edit a macro.

You have developed a macro that applies multiple formats to the contents of a cell. One of the formats sets the font size in the cell to 12 point; however, you meant to set the point size to 16. All the other settings in the macro work fine. Would you rather rerecord the entire macro and risk making an error in the recording, or would you rather edit the existing macro and change the 12 point value to 16? Editing macros eliminates the need to rerecord complex macros in situations where most of a macro works appropriately.

Visual Basic for Applications (VBA)

Visual Basic for Applications (VBA) is the programming language used to create macros in Microsoft Office 2007 applications. When you record a macro, Excel automatically translates the keystrokes and commands into VBA code language, and creates and stores the macro.

 If you are familiar with the VBA programming language and syntax, you can create macros directly in VBA.

VBA Modules

Each macro consists of a block of VBA code. Macro code is grouped in larger VBA code blocks known as *modules*. Documents and templates can contain one or more modules, and modules can contain one or more macros.

The Visual Basic Editor

The *Visual Basic Editor* is an add-in application you can use to load, view, and edit the VBA code for a macro. The application window has its own interface, menu bar, and Help system.

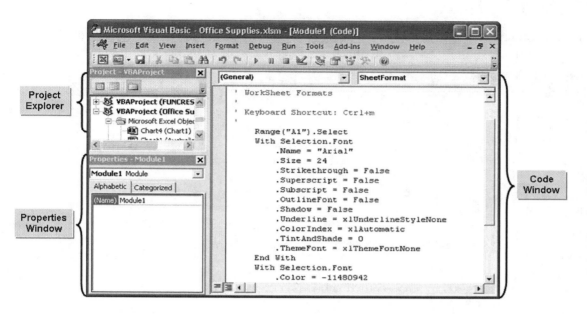

Figure 1-2: *A macro code block in the Visual Basic Editor window.*

The Visual Basic Editor window is made up of various components.

Microsoft Visual Basic Editor Window Component	Description
Project Explorer	A hierarchical interface listing VBA modules in all open documents and templates. The normal template is listed as Normal. Open documents appear as Project objects. Open templates appear as TemplateProject objects.
Properties Window	Lists the properties of whatever object is selected in the Project Explorer. A property is a characteristic of the object. For example, one property of a VBA module is the module's name.
Code Window	Displays the VBA code of the selected project for editing.

Macro Settings

In order to protect macros, you can set security levels to them. You can view or change the macro security level in the Macro Settings category of the Trust Center dialog box.

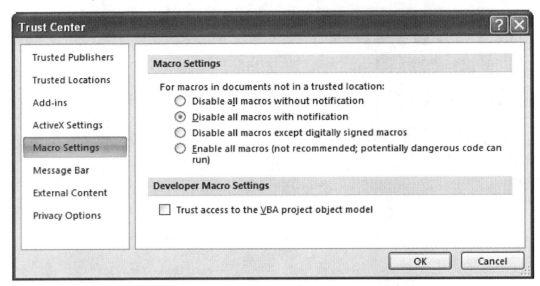

Figure 1-3: The different macro settings in the Trust Center dialog box.

Option	Description
Disable All Macros Without Notification	Disables all macros in the workbook and their security alerts. Documents stored in a trusted location containing macros are allowed to run.
Disable All Macros With Notification	Disables all macros but not their security alerts. This is the default setting. This setting allows you to choose which macros to run.
Disable All Macros Except Digitally Signed Macros	Disables all macros except those that are digitally signed by a trusted publisher.
Enable all Macros (Not Recommended, Potentially Dangerous Code Can Run)	Enables all macros in the workbook to run. This lowers the security of the computer, making it vulnerable to malicious code. This option is not recommended as it may allow potentially dangerous code in the macro to run.
Trust Access To The VBA Project Object Model	Enables macros to access the core Microsoft Visual Basic objects, methods, and properties. This option is for developers only, as it poses a security hazard.

How to Edit a Macro

Procedure Reference: Adjust Macro Settings

To adjust macro settings:

1. In the Excel Options dialog box, in the Trust Center category, in the Microsoft Office Excel Trust Center section, click Trust Center Settings to display the Trust Center dialog box.
2. In the Trust Center dialog box, select the level of macro security you desire.
3. Click OK to save the macro security settings.
4. Close the Excel Options dialog box.

Procedure Reference: Edit a Macro

To edit a macro:

1. Open the worksheet with the macro you want to edit.
2. If necessary, enable macros in a document.
   a. In the Security Warning panel, click Options.
   b. In the Microsoft Office Security Options dialog box, select the Enable This Content option and click OK.
3. On the View tab, in the Macros group, from the Macros drop-down list, select View Macros.
4. In the Macro dialog box, in the Macro Name list box, select the macro you want to edit and click Edit.
5. Make the changes to the macro in the corresponding code window of the macro.
6. Return to Excel.
7. Apply the newly edited macro.
8. Save the file.

ACTIVITY 1-2

Editing a Macro

Before You Begin:

My Office Supplies.xlsm is open.

Scenario:

You have created your macro, but now there are a few things you would like to change:

- The font size you chose for cell A1 is too big.

- The range of cells that the macro converts to bold and italics should be B3:E3 rather than A3:E3.

- The contents of cell A3 should not appear in bold or italics.

You do not want to waste time in rerecording the entire macro. You just want to make these changes.

What You Do	How You Do It
1. Open the SheetFormat macro in the Visual Basic Editor.	a. On the View tab, in the Macros group, **click the Macros drop-down arrow and select View Macros.**
	b. In the Macro dialog box, **verify that SheetFormat is selected by default and click Edit** to open the macro in the Visual Basic Editor.

2. **Edit the macro to decrease the font size for cell A1 to 14 points.**

   a. In the My Office Supplies.xlsm - [Module1 (Code)] window, on the `.Size` line of the `With` statement, **double-click 24** to select it.

```
Range("A1").Select
With Selection.Font
    .Name = "Arial"
    .Size = 24
    .Strikethrough = False
    .Superscript = False
    .Subscript = False
    .OutlineFont = False
    .Shadow = False
    .Underline = xlUnderlineStyleNone
    .ColorIndex = xlAutomatic
    .TintAndShade = 0
    .ThemeFont = xlThemeFontNone
End With
```

   b. **Type 14**

3. **Edit the macro to change the range of cells that appear in bold and italics from A3:E3 to B3:E3.**

   a. Observe the first `Range` line of code that follows the `End With` statement and **select A3.**

```
End With
Range("A3:E3").Select
Selection.Font.Bold = True
Selection.Font.Italic = True
Range("B4:E9").Select
Selection.Style = "Currency"
End Sub
```

   b. **Type B3**

4. **Edit the macro to remove the bold and italics formatting from cell A3.**

a. **Select the lines of code from** `Range("B3:E3")` **to** `Selection.Font.Italic = True` **which applies bold and italics formatting to the B3:E3 range.**

```
       End With
       Range("B3:E3").Select
       Selection.Font.Bold = True
       Selection.Font.Italic = True
       Range("B4:E9").Select
       Selection.Style = "Currency"
   End Sub
```

b. **Choose Edit→Copy.**

c. **Click at the end of the selected code and press Enter** to create a new line to add the copied code.

d. **Choose Edit→Paste.**

e. In the newly pasted code, on the `Range` line, **select** `B3:E3` **and type** *A3*

```
       Range("B3:E3").Select
       Selection.Font.Bold = True
       Selection.Font.Italic = True
       Range("A3").Select
       Selection.Font.Bold = True
       Selection.Font.Italic = True
       Range("B4:E9").Select
       Selection.Style = "Currency"
   End Sub
```

f. In the newly pasted code, on the line of code that begins with `Selection.Font.Bold`, **double-click** `True` **and type** `False`

g. In the newly pasted code, on the line of code that begins with `Selection.Font.Italic`, **select** `True` **and type** `False`

```
       Range("B3:E3").Select
       Selection.Font.Bold = True
       Selection.Font.Italic = True
       Range("A3").Select
       Selection.Font.Bold = False
       Selection.Font.Italic = False
       Range("B4:E9").Select
       Selection.Style = "Currency"
   End Sub
```

5. **Return to the Worksheet view, and update the Australian worksheet with the new macro.**

a. **Click the View Microsoft Office Excel button** to return to the workbook.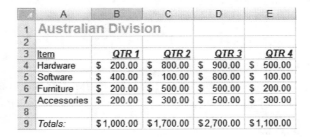

b. In the New Office Supplies.xlsm file, **select the Australian worksheet tab.**

c. **Press Ctrl+M** to apply the updated macro to the sheet.

d. Observe that the edited format has been applied to the worksheet.

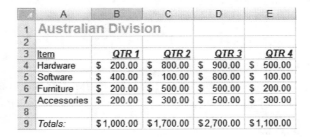

	A	B	C	D	E
1	Australian Division				
2					
3	Item	*QTR 1*	*QTR 2*	*QTR 3*	*QTR 4*
4	Hardware	$ 200.00	$ 800.00	$ 900.00	$ 500.00
5	Software	$ 400.00	$ 100.00	$ 800.00	$ 100.00
6	Furniture	$ 200.00	$ 500.00	$ 500.00	$ 200.00
7	Accessories	$ 200.00	$ 300.00	$ 500.00	$ 300.00
8					
9	*Totals:*	$1,000.00	$1,700.00	$2,700.00	$1,100.00

e. **Save the file as** *My New Office Supplies.xlsm* **and close it.**

f. **Restore and close the Microsoft Visual Basic window.**

TOPIC C
Apply Conditional Formatting

You have automated tasks you frequently perform on a worksheet. You have data in a worksheet and you want to change the data's appearance based upon the criteria you set. In this topic, you will apply conditional formatting.

Conditionally formatting data makes it easier to quickly identify specific information that meets a given criterion. A worksheet with conditional formatting applied will make it easier to identify and differentiate between the data within it.

Conditional Formatting

Definition:

Conditional formatting is a formatting technique that applies a specified format to a cell or range of cells based upon a set of predefined criteria. In Excel, the cells to be formatted can contain numeric or textual data. The condition for formatting can be set using default or user-defined rules.

Example:

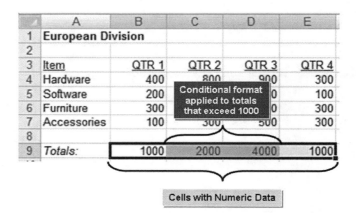

Conditional Formats

Excel provides different types of conditional formats that can be applied using the Conditional Formatting option in the Styles group on the Home tab.

Format	Description
Highlight Cell Rules	This format is used to quickly find specific cells within a range of cells. You can format those specific cells based on a comparison operator. This format is applied by selecting the desired option displayed in the Highlight Cell Rules submenu.
Top/Bottom Rules	This format is used to find the highest and lowest values in a range of cells based on a cutoff value you specify. This format is applied by selecting the desired option in the Top/Bottom Rules submenu.

Format	Description
Data Bars	This format is used to view the value of a cell relative to other cells. The length of the data bar represents the value in the cell. This format is applied by selecting a data bar format from the Data Bars gallery. A data bar can be customized if required.
Color Scales	This format is used to visually represent data distribution and variation. The shade of the color in this format represents higher, middle, or lower values. This format is applied by selecting a color scale format from the Color Scales gallery. A color scale can be customized if required.
Icon Sets	This format is used to annotate and classify data into three to five categories. Each category is represented by an icon. This format is applied by selecting an icon set type from the Icon Sets gallery. An icon set can be customized if required.

The Conditional Formatting Rules Manager Dialog Box

The Conditional Formatting Rules Manager dialog box is used to define one or more conditional format rules for data sets. This dialog box can be used to create, edit, and delete a rule. It also lists all the rules in a worksheet.

How to Apply Conditional Formatting

Procedure Reference: Apply Conditional Formatting

To apply conditional formatting:

1. Select the cell or cells to which you want to apply the formatting.
2. On the Home tab, in the Styles group, click Conditional Formatting.
3. From the Conditional Formatting drop-down list, select a conditional format type.
   - Choose an option from the Highlight Cell Rules submenu to highlight cells using comparison values.
   - Choose an option from the Top/Bottom Rules submenu to highlight cells using the highest 10 or lowest 10 values.
   - Choose a data bar type from the Data Bars submenu to format cells using relative values.
   - Choose a color scale type from the Color Scales submenu to format cells using distribution and variation values.
   - Choose an icon set type from the Icon Sets submenu to format cells using categorized values.

Procedure Reference: Create a New Conditional Formatting Rule

To create a new conditional formatting rule:

1. On the Home tab, in the Styles group, click Conditional Formatting.

2. Display the New Formatting Rules dialog box.

   - Display the New Formatting Rules dialog box using the Conditional Formatting Rules Manager dialog box.

     a. Select Manage Rules.

     b. In the Conditional Formatting Rules Manager dialog box, if necessary, select an option from the Show Formatting Rules For drop-down list to display all the rules in a particular location.

     c. Click New Rule.

   - Or, from the Conditional Formatting drop-down list, select New Rule.

3. In the Select A Rule Type section, select the desired option.

4. In the Edit The Rule Description section, format the cells based on their values.

   - From the Format Style drop-down list, select a format style.

   - From the Minimum and Maximum Type drop-down lists, select a value type of Lowest Value, Number, Percent, Formula, or Percentile.

   - In the Minimum and Maximum Value text boxes, select or enter a value.

   - From the Color drop-down lists, select a color for the minimum and maximum values.

5. Preview the format.

6. Click OK to apply the new conditional format.

Procedure Reference: Edit an Existing Conditional Formatting Rule

To edit an existing conditional formatting rule:

1. On the Home tab, in the Styles group, from the Conditional Formatting drop-down list, select Manage Rules.

2. In the Conditional Formatting Rules Manager dialog box, if necessary, select an option from the Show Formatting Rules For drop-down list to display all the rules in a particular location.

3. In the Rule pane, select the rule you want to edit.

4. Click Edit Rule.

5. In the Edit Formatting Rule dialog box, edit the properties and settings of the rules.

6. Click OK to close the Edit Formatting Rule dialog box.

7. In the Conditional Formatting Rules Manager dialog box, click OK to update the rule for the data.

Procedure Reference: Delete a Conditional Formatting Rule

To delete a conditional formatting rule:

1. On the Home tab, in the Styles group, from the Conditional Formatting drop-down list, select Manage Rules.

2. If necessary, select an option from the Show Formatting Rules For drop-down list to display all the rules in a particular location.

3. In the Conditional Formatting Rules Manager dialog box, in the Rule pane, select the rule you want to delete.

4. Click Delete Rule to delete the conditional formatting rule.

Procedure Reference: Sort Data Using Conditional Formatting

To sort data using conditional formatting:

1. On the Home tab, in the Editing group, click Sort & Filter.
2. From the Sort & Filter drop-down list, click Custom Sort.
3. In the Sort dialog box, from the Sort By drop-down list, select the column you want to sort.
4. From the Sort drop-down list, select the type of sort.
   - Select Values to sort by cell value.
   - Select Cell Color to sort by cell color.
   - Select Font Color to sort by font color.
   - Select Cell Icon to sort by an icon set.
5. From the Order drop-down list, select the order option in which you would like to sort.
6. If necessary, click Add Level, and specify the value, cell color, font color, or cell icon for the next sort level.
7. Click OK to sort the data.

Procedure Reference: Filter Data Using Conditional Formatting

To filter data using conditional formatting:

1. Select the column to which conditional formatting has been applied.
2. On the Home tab, in the Editing group, click Sort & Filter.
3. From the Sort & Filter drop-down list, click Filter to display the arrow in the column header.
4. Click the column header filter drop-down arrow, and from the Filter By Color submenu, choose the color by which you want to filter the column.

ACTIVITY 1-3
Creating a Conditional Format

Data Files:

Office Supplies Format.xlsx

Before You Begin:

From the C:\084892Data\Streamlining Workflow folder, open Office Supplies Format.xlsx.

Scenario:

The Office Supplies Format workbook summarizes the total amount spent on office supplies in the three divisions of your company. Because of budget constraints, anyone in the Australian division who is spending more than $1,500 in a quarter needs to be notified. You want to highlight the cells that exceed the amount of $1,500 in green to draw attention to those numbers.

What You Do	How You Do It
1. Select the range displaying the totals of each quarter in the Australian worksheet tab.	a. Select the Australian worksheet tab.
	b. Select the range B9:E9.
2. Apply a condition to the Australian quarterly totals, so that any total that exceeds $1500.00 will be formatted in green.	a. On the Home tab, in the Styles group, click Conditional Formatting and then choose Highlight Cells Rules→Greater Than.
	b. In the Greater Than dialog box, type *1500*
	c. From the With drop-down list, select Green Fill With Dark Green Text and click OK.

| | d. Save the file as *My Office Supplies Format.xlsx* and close it. |

ACTIVITY 1-4

Editing Conditional Formats

Data Files:

Product Sales.xlsx

Before You Begin:

From the C:\084892Data\Streamlining Workflow folder, open Product Sales.xlsx.

Scenario:

On the Summary worksheet of the Product Sales workbook, you have applied the data bar type of conditional formatting to the Totals data. You want to make the formatting more prominent by applying a two color scale type that has orange for lower values and yellow for higher values.

Also, in the B&B - Product Sales worksheet, you notice that you have applied similar conditional formatting for quarterly sales and annual sales. You do not want the Annual Totals to be formatted.

What You Do	How You Do It
1. Modify the rule for a data bar conditional format.	a. **Verify that the Summary worksheet tab is selected.**
	b. On the Home tab, in the Styles group, **click Conditional Formatting, and select Manage Rules.**
	c. In the Conditional Formatting Rules Manager dialog box, from the Show Formatting Rules For drop-down list, **select This Worksheet.**
	d. **Click Edit Rule** to display the Edit Formatting Rule dialog box.
	e. In the Edit Formatting Rule dialog box, in the Edit The Rule Description section, from the Format Style drop-down list, **select 2-Color Scale.**

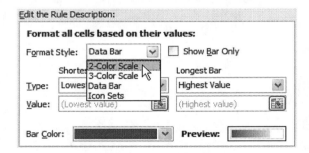

	f. Observe that the color for the highest value is yellow and the lowest is orange.
	g. In the Edit Formatting Rule dialog box, **click OK** to close it.
	h. In the Conditional Formatting Rules Manager dialog box, **click OK** to apply the formatting to the data set.
2. Display the conditional format rule applied to the Annual Sales column in the worksheet.	a. **Select the B&B - Product Sales worksheet tab.**
	b. **Scroll to the right** to move to the Annual Totals column.
	c. **Select the range R5:R12.**
	d. In the Styles group, **click the Conditional Formatting drop-down arrow and select Manage Rules.**

3. **Delete the rule for the Annual Totals column.**

   a. In the Conditional Formatting Rules Manager dialog box, in the Rule pane, **select the Graded Color Scale rule.**

   b. **Click Delete Rule** to remove the rule from the Rule pane.

   c. **Click OK** to delete the conditional formatting from the Annual Totals column.

   d. Observe that the formatting applied to the Annual Totals column has been removed.

   e. **Save the file as *My Product Sales.xlsx***

ACTIVITY 1-5

Sorting and Filtering Conditionally Formatted Data

Before You Begin:

My Product Sales.xlsx is open.

Scenario:

You want to group the total monthly sales data in the B&B – Total Sales by Month worksheet of the workbook based on the color format applied to it. After grouping the data, you only want data of a certain format to be present in the workbook.

What You Do	How You Do It
1. Sort the data with high sale values on top and low sale values at the bottom.	a. Select the **B&B - Total Sales By Month** worksheet tab.
	b. Observe that a pink format has been applied to sales data over $970.
	c. In the Editing group, **click the Sort & Filter drop-down arrow, and select Custom Sort.**
	d. In the Sort dialog box, from the Sort By drop-down list, **select (Column B).**
	e. From the Sort On drop-down list, **select Cell Color.**
	f. **Verify that pink is displayed in the Order drop-down list box and that the cells with the particular color will appear on top.**
	g. **Click OK** to sort the data.
2. Filter only the data with the green font format.	a. In the Editing group, **click Sort & Filter, and select Filter.**

b. **Click the drop-down arrow in the Column B heading,** and from the menu, **choose Filter By Color.**

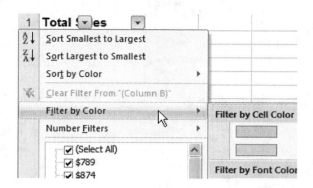

c. From the Filter By Color submenu, in the Filter By Cell Color section, **select the green color** to filter the data.

d. **Save the file as** *My Sort Product Sales.xlsx* **and close it.**

TOPIC D
Add Data Validation Criteria

You have worked with worksheets that store various types of data. You now want to force certain cells in the worksheet to accept only a specific type of data. In this topic, you will add a data validation criterion.

You are developing a worksheet with a column that must contain values that can only be in the range of 100 to 1500. You decide to add a data validation rule which will force any value in the column to fall within the specified range. Adding data validation criteria helps improve the integrity of your data by forcing specified cells to accept only a specific type of data.

Data Validation

Definition:

Data validation is a technique used to restrict the value or type of data that can be given as input based on a specific set of criteria. Cells that have had data validation criteria applied to them can only take data that meets the validation criteria. Any attempt to store data of a type other than that defined by the criteria will result in an error message.

Data validation can include a user-defined input message which indicates to users the type of data that the cell or range can contain. Data validation can be applied to a cell or range of cells.

Example:

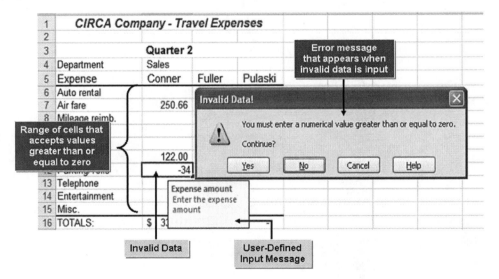

The Data Validation Dialog Box

The Data Validation dialog box has three tabs to specify the settings, input message, and error alert for data that can be entered in a cell.

Tab	Function
Settings	Allows the user to set the permitted value type such as decimal, date, and time. The range of data that can be entered in a cell is also set here. It is also possible to create a drop-down list by using the options on this tab.
Input Message	Allows the user to set a specific title and description of data to be entered in a cell.
Error Alert	Allows the user to specify a style, title, and description of an error alert that pops up if the input data does not meet the specified criteria.

How to Add Data Validation Criteria

Procedure Reference: Add a Data Validation Rule

To add a data validation rule:

1. In an Excel worksheet, select the range to which you want to apply data validation.
2. On the Data tab, in the Data Tools group, click Data Validation.
3. In the Data Validation dialog box, on the Settings tab, set the criteria for a valid entry.
   - From the Allow drop-down list, select the type of validation you want.
   - From the Data drop-down list, select a comparison operator.
   - In the Minimum and/or Maximum text boxes, set the desired values for valid data entries.
4. On the Input Message tab, create an optional message.
   - In the Title text box, type a title for the message.
   - In the Input Message text area, type the required message.
5. If necessary, on the Error Alert tab, make changes to the default error message.
   - From the Style drop-down list, select an error icon.
   - In the Title text box, type a title for the error message.
   - In the Error Message text area, type the desired error message.
6. Click OK to add data validation.
7. Test the data validation rule.

Procedure Reference: Create a Drop-Down List from a Range of Cells

To create a drop-down list from a range of cells:

1. In an Excel workbook, create a list of valid entries for the drop-down list.
2. Select the range of valid entries.
3. At the left end of the Formula bar, in the Name text box, type a name for the selected list.
4. Select the cell where the drop-down list should appear.

5. In the Data Validation dialog box, select the Settings tab.

6. From the Allow drop-down list, select List.

7. In the Source text box, type the equals sign and enter the reference name in the list you created. All the items in the reference list will become part of the drop-down list.

8. Verify that the In-cell Drop-down check box is checked to ensure that the drop-down arrow will appear within the cell.

9. If necessary, on the Input Message tab, create a message.

10. If necessary, on the Error Alert tab, create a message for invalid data entries.

11. Click OK.

ACTIVITY 1-6
Adding Data Validation Rules

Data Files:

Monthly Expenses.xlsx

Before You Begin:

From the C:\084892Data\Streamlining Workflow folder, open Monthly Expenses.xlsx.

Scenario:

You are creating a workbook that tracks monthly travel expenses for employees. In order to ensure that the data in the workbook remains valid, you decide to impose the following restrictions to the data in the range of cells that store the expense values.

● Force any cell in the range to accept only numerical values less than 10000.

● Label each cell in the range with a short note explaining the type of data the cells can store.

● Return an error message if a user tries to enter a nonnumeric value into any cell in the range.

● Allow the user to select a valid entry from a drop-down list.

● Restrict the destination name entered to six letters.

What You Do	How You Do It
1. **Set the validation criteria to accept decimal values less than 10000 for the range B7:D16.**	a. **Select the range B7:D16.**
	b. On the Data tab, in the Data Tools group, **click Data Validation** to display the Data Validation dialog box.
	c. In the Data Validation dialog box, on the Settings tab, from the Allow drop-down list, **select Decimal.**
	d. From the Data drop-down list, **select Less Than.**

e. In the Maximum text box, **type** *10000*

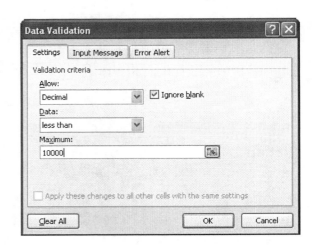

2. **Set a message that will display on any cell of the selected range.**

  a. In the Data Validation dialog box, **select the Input Message tab.**

  b. In the Title text box, **type** *Expense Amount*

  c. In the Input Message text area, **type** *Enter the expense amount*

3. **Set the error alert for invalid data.**

  a. In the Data Validation dialog box, **select the Error Alert tab.**

  b. Observe that the Show Error Alert After Invalid Data Is Entered check box is checked by default.

  c. From the Style drop-down list, **select Warning.**

  d. In the Title text box, **type** *Invalid Data!*

  e. In the Error Message text area, **type** *You must enter a numerical value less than 10000*

  f. **Click OK** to add the data validation rule.

4.	Create a drop-down list for entering a valid department name.	a.	**Click cell B5.**
		b.	**Display the Data Validation dialog box.**
		c.	In the Data Validation dialog box, on the Settings tab, from the Allow drop-down list, **select List.**
		d.	In the Source text box, **type *=Dept* and click OK** to create the drop-down list.
5.	Create a data validation rule that restricts the length of characters allowed in a cell to six.	a.	**Click cell B3**.
		b.	**Display the Data Validation dialog box.**
		c.	On the Settings tab, from the Allow drop-down list, **select Text Length.**
		d.	From the Data drop-down list, **select Less Than Or Equal To.**
		e.	In the Maximum text box, **type *6***
		f.	On the Input Message tab, in the Input Message text area, **type *Enter a destination name with six or fewer characters.***
		g.	**Click OK** to apply the data validation rule.
6.	Test the data validation rules.	a.	Observe that the input message is already available for the selected cell.
		b.	In cell B3, **type *NewYork* and press Enter.**
		c.	In the Microsoft Office Excel message box, **click Retry.**
		d.	**Type *NY* and press Enter** to enter valid data into the cell.
		e.	**Click cell B5** to view the drop-down arrow, and from the drop-down list, **select Sales** to test the drop-down list.
		f.	**Click cell B7.**

g. Observe that the input message is already
    visible for the selected cell.

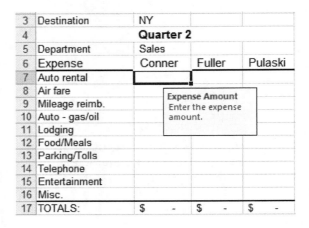

3	Destination	NY		
4		**Quarter 2**		
5	Department	Sales		
6	Expense	Conner	Fuller	Pulaski
7	Auto rental			
8	Air fare			
9	Mileage reimb.			
10	Auto - gas/oil			
11	Lodging			
12	Food/Meals			
13	Parking/Tolls			
14	Telephone			
15	Entertainment			
16	Misc.			
17	TOTALS:	$ -	$ -	$ -

h. In cell B7 *type 10500* **and then press
    Enter** to view the error alert.

i. In the Invalid Data! warning box that
    states whether you want to continue, **click
    No.**

j. In cell B7, **type** *250.66* **and press Enter**
    to enter valid data into the cell.

k. **Save the file as** *My Monthly
    Expenses.xlsx* **and close it.**

TOPIC E
Update a Workbook's Properties

You have identified information within a workbook by applying conditional formatting. Now you need to identify a workbook with specific information, such as a title and summary, that enables you to easily locate the workbook. In this topic, you will update a workbook's properties.

Roberta Williams, a human resources manager, has come to you hoping you can find a workbook you developed over a year ago. She knows the contents of the file, but she can't find it. She knows Steve Wooten was the project manager who used the workbook; however, Steve has left the company. You run a search through your backup directories looking for all files that include the name Steve Wooten in the Manager property. It takes only a few moments for you to locate the required file. By updating a workbook's properties, you can attach specific information to a workbook which makes it easier to locate the file on a computer and identify the file's contents.

Workbook Properties

In Excel, the Document Information panel is used to specify information that helps to identify or describe the workbook. In this panel, when you select Advanced Properties from the Document Properties drop-down list, the [Document Name] Properties dialog box is displayed.

The Properties dialog box contains five tabs of information regarding the opened file.

Tab	Description
General	Identifies the file's name, type, location, size, MS-DOS name, creation, modification, access dates, and attributes such as whether the file is read-only. You cannot alter this information from within the Properties dialog box. The system supplies this information.
Summary	Allows you to specify the file's title, subject, author, manager, company, category, keywords, and hyperlink base.
Statistics	Lists system information such as the creation date, last modified date, last accessed date, and last printed date. It also identifies the name of the person the file was last saved by, the revision number (if applicable), and the total editing time (if applicable). The data on this tab cannot be edited.
Contents	Identifies the total number of worksheets by name. The data on this tab cannot be edited.
Custom	Allows you to attach specific information to the file, such as the destination, editor, language, and so on. Apart from the suggested options available on the tab, it is possible to add a property name of your own.

How to Update a Workbook's Properties

Procedure Reference: Update a Workbook's Properties

To update a workbook's properties:

1. Open the [Document Name] Properties dialog box.

   - In the open workbook, click the Office button, choose Prepare→Properties, and in the Document Information panel, from the Document Properties drop-down list, select Advanced Properties.

   - For an unopened workbook, in the Open dialog box, select the desired file, and from the Tools drop-down list box, select Properties.

   - Or, click the Office button, select Save As, and in the Save As dialog box, select Properties from the Tools pop-up menu.

2. Modify the desired properties.

   - On the Summary tab, specify the necessary details in the respective text boxes.

   - On the Custom tab, specify the custom properties.

     a. Either select an existing name in the Name list box or type a new name in the Name text box to specify a name for the custom property.

     b. If necessary, from the Type drop-down list, select Text, Date, Number, or Yes Or No, to limit the type of value that can be entered.

     c. In the Value text box, type the value of the custom property. If you selected Yes Or No from the Type drop-down list, select the Yes or Not option.

     d. Click Add.

    The Link To Content check box allows you to store the custom property in an existing bookmark within the document.

3. Click OK to close the [Document Name] Properties dialog box.

4. Save the document to store the new properties with the file.

ACTIVITY 1-7

Updating a Workbook's Properties

Data Files:

Sales Data Canada.xlsx

Before You Begin:

From the C:\084892Data\Streamlining Workflow folder, open Sales Data Canada.xlsx.

Scenario:

Josh Duvane recently began developing a workbook titled Sales Data Canada. However, Josh was recently reassigned to a new group in your company and was unable to finish development on the workbook. His manager, Roberta Williams, wants to identify the file as "Sales Data – Canada." She also wants her name listed as the manager of the file, Josh's name as the author of the file, and Mary Coleman's name listed as the editor of the file. Additionally, she would like to be able to easily locate the file using words like "Canada," "Sales," and "Vendor Code."

What You Do	How You Do It
1. Add a title to the workbook.	a. **Click the Office button and choose Prepare→Properties.**
	b. In the Document Information panel, **click Document Properties, and select Advanced Properties.**
	c. In the Sales Data Canada.xlsx Properties dialog box, **select the Summary tab.**
	d. In the Title text box, type ***Sales Data-Canada***
2. Add the author name, manager name, and keywords to the file.	a. In the Author text box, **type *Josh Duvane***
	b. In the Manager text box, **type *Roberta Williams***
	c. In the Keywords text box, **type *Canada, Sales, Vendor Code***

3.	Add a custom property noting Mary Coleman as the editor of the file.	a.	**Select the Custom tab.**
		b.	In the Name list box, **select Editor.**
		c.	**Verify that Text is selected by default in the Type drop-down list box.**
		d.	In the Value text box, **type *Mary Coleman***
		e.	**Click Add** to display the modified editor details in the Properties area and **click OK.**
		f.	**Save the document as *My Sales Data Canada* and close it.**
4.	View the properties of the updated file without opening it.	a.	**Display the Open dialog box.**
		b.	**If necessary, navigate to C:\084892Data\ Streamlining Workflow.**
		c.	**Select My Sales Data Canada.xslx.**
		d.	**Click Tools and select Properties.**
		e.	In the My Sales Data Canada.xlsx Properties dialog box, **select the Summary tab.**
		f.	**Verify that the updated Summary details were added.**
		g.	On the Custom tab, **verify that the updated Custom details were added and click OK.**
		h.	**Click Cancel** to close the Open dialog box.
		i.	**Close the Document Information panel.**

TOPIC F

Modify Excel's Default Settings

You have updated the properties of a workbook in Excel. You want to make changes to some of Excel's default settings so that you don't repeatedly find yourself adjusting it every time you work with Excel. In this topic, you will modify Excel's default settings.

Every time you open Excel and create a new file, the application defaults to Times New Roman. However, your organization uses Verdana as it is the font of choice for all internal and external communications. Though it is not too difficult to change the font each time, it would however be easier if all new files automatically started in Verdana. You can do this by changing Excel's default settings. By modifying Excel's default settings, you can streamline your workflow by forcing Excel to use settings you have defined to meet your current business needs.

How to Modify Excel's Default Settings

Procedure Reference: Modify Excel's Default Settings

To modify Excel's default settings:

1. Click the Office button and then click Excel Options.
2. In the Excel Options dialog box, select the Popular category.
3. In the When Creating New Workbooks section, from the Use This Font drop-down list, select the font you want to use as the default font.
4. From the Font Size drop-down list, select the font size you want to set as the default font.
5. If desired, from the Default View For New Sheets drop-down list, select the preferred default view.
6. In the Include This Many Sheets spin box, specify a value for the number of sheets to be displayed in a workbook and click OK. By default, 255 is the maximum number of worksheets a workbook can contain.
7. In the Microsoft Excel warning box that states you must quit and restart Excel, click OK.
8. Close Excel.
9. Open Excel to test the updated default settings.

Procedure Reference: Change the Default File Storage Location

To change the default file storage location:

1. If necessary, create a folder in the location where you want to store the files by default.
2. Display the Excel Options dialog box.
3. In the Excel Options dialog box, select the Save category.
4. In the Default File Location text box, type the path where you want to save the files.
5. In the Excel Options dialog box, click OK.

ACTIVITY 1-8

Modifying Excel's Default Settings

Before You Begin:

No files are open.

Scenario:

You are in the process of setting up your Excel environment for a new project. You know that every workbook you create for this project will have a minimum of five worksheets and that all of the text for each workbook must appear in size 12 point with Courier New font. Because you want to keep the files for this project separate from other Excel files on your computer, you have decided to create a new folder named My Project Files in the My Documents folder.

What You Do	How You Do It
1. **Set the default number of sheets in a new workbook to five.**	a. **Open a new, blank workbook.**
	b. **Click the Office button and then click Excel Options.**
	c. In the Excel Options dialog box, with the Popular category selected, in the When Creating New Workbooks section, in the Include This Many Sheets spin box, **click the up arrow two times** to set the value to 5.
2. **Set the default font style and size to Courier New and 12, respectively.**	a. From the Use This Font drop-down list, **select Courier New.**
	b. From the Font Size drop-down list, **select 12.**
	c. **Click OK.**
	d. In the Microsoft Excel warning box that states you will have to quit and restart Excel for the changes to take effect, **click OK.**

3.	Create a new folder called My Project Files in the My Documents folder.	a.	In Windows Explorer, **navigate to My Documents.**
		b.	In the right pane of the window, **right-click and choose New→Folder.**
		c.	**Name the new folder** *My Project Files* **and press Enter.**
		d.	**Close the My Documents window.**
4.	Change the default location to save the Excel workbooks to the My Project Files folder in My Documents.	a.	**Click the Office button and then click Excel Options.**
		b.	In the Excel Options dialog box, **select the Save category.**
		c.	In the Save Workbooks section, in the Default File Location text box, after the existing path, **type *My Project Files*
		d.	**Click OK.**
5.	Test your work.	a.	**Restart Excel.**
		b.	In cell A1, **type** *house* to confirm that the font style is Courier New and the font size is 12.
		c.	At the bottom of the workbook, **verify that there are five worksheet tabs in the new file.**
		d.	**Click the Office button and choose Save As.**
		e.	In the Save In drop-down list, **verify that the My Project Files folder appears by default.**
		f.	In the Save As dialog box, **click Cancel.**
		g.	**Close the file without saving.**

Lesson 1 Follow-up

In this lesson, you streamlined your workflow and increased your productivity by tailoring the Excel environment to your job needs.

1. **Consider the Excel projects on which you have worked. What types of macros would have helped to increase your productivity with these projects?**

2. **What projects are you currently working on that would benefit from conditional formatting and data validation? How might you apply conditional formatting and data validation to these projects?**

2 | Collaborating with Others

Lesson Time: 1 hour(s), 20 minutes

Lesson Objectives:

In this lesson, you will collaborate with others using workbooks.

You will:

- Protect files.
- Share a workbook.
- Set revision tracking.
- Review tracked revisions.
- Merge workbooks.
- Administer digital signatures.
- Restrict document access.

Introduction

You worked by yourself on the development of Microsoft® Office Excel® workbooks. You would now like to include other people in the development process. In this lesson, you will collaborate with others.

In a work environment, there are instances where you may have to coordinate with others to work on a common file. While collaborating with other users, you make your data available to others, and they make their data available to you.

TOPIC A
Protect Files

You streamlined your workflow to help you work efficiently. Now you have some Excel files you would like to share with others, while ensuring that the data in the files is safe. In this topic, you will protect files.

You have a workbook that other users in your organization need to read. However, you don't want anyone to alter the data or layout of the workbook in any way. Before sharing the workbook, you decide to protect it so the other users will have read-only access. Protecting files gives you the flexibility to share them knowing that the data is secure.

The Collaboration Process

The collaboration process to share Excel workbooks with other users involves four stages: protecting, saving, sharing, and reviewing.

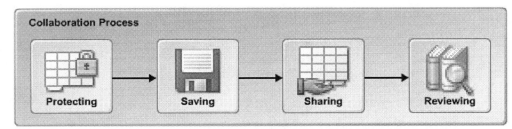

Figure 2-1: Various stages in the collaboration process.

Stage	Description
Protecting	In this stage, users protect the worksheet to ensure that other users do not alter the elements in the sheet.
Saving	In this stage, users save the workbook as a shared workbook to allow multiple users to make changes to the file at the same time.
Sharing	In this stage, users share the workbook to allow other users to make changes.
Reviewing	In this stage, users review the workbook to view and incorporate the changes made by others.

File Protection

Excel has two different security options you can use to protect information contained in workbooks: authorized opening of a workbook and authorized modification of a workbook. Additionally, you can protect the worksheet structure and window layout of workbooks from other users by setting a password. Users without the password are blocked from either moving worksheets around in a workbook or altering the display of windows in a workbook.

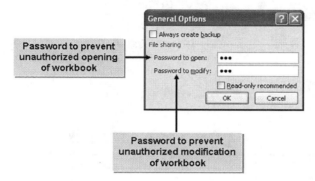

Figure 2-2: The file protection options in the General Options dialog box.

The Changes Group

The Changes group on the Review tab of the Ribbon has options to protect, share, edit, and track changes in a worksheet or a workbook.

Option	Description
Protect Sheet	Allows you to specify the options that help to protect a worksheet.
Protect Workbook	Prevents new sheets from being created and limits access of the workbook to specific users.
Share Workbook	Allows different users to access a workbook at the same time. The workbook needs to be saved in a network. However, a workbook with tables cannot be shared. Either worksheets with tables need to be converted to ranges, or XML mapping needs to be removed.
Protect And Share Workbook	Allows you to protect a workbook, and at the same time share it among multiple users on the network. The workbook can be protected by specifying a password, and this prevents users from turning off track changing.
Allow Users To Edit Ranges	Allows users to edit ranges of protected cells. This option can be used only if the computer is connected to a Microsoft Windows domain.
Track Changes	Allows you to track all changes made to the workbook.

The Protect Workbook Option

The Protect Workbook option in the Changes group of the Review tab allows you to restrict permission to edit and access a workbook. This option, in turn, holds a drop-down list of other options that allow you to protect the workbook.

Option	*Description*
Protect Structure And Windows	Displays the Protect Structure And Windows dialog box which allows you to protect the structure of the workbook, and ensures that the workbook window always opens in the same size and position.
Unrestricted Access	Allows all users to modify the workbook.
Restricted Access	Allows only specified users to modify the workbook.
Manage Credentials	Allows you to change logon credentials.

How to Protect Files

Procedure Reference: Protect Worksheets

To protect worksheets:

1. Set the desired protection level in the Format Cells dialog box.

    a. Select the range of cells you want to lock.

    b. On the Home tab, in the Cells group, from the Format drop-down list, select Format Cells.

    c. In the Format Cells dialog box, select the Protection tab.

    d. On the Protection tab, lock or hide the selected range of cells.

    - Check the Locked check box to lock the cells.

    - Check the Hidden check box to hide the formulas in the cells.

    e. Click OK to close the dialog box and save the settings.

2. Set the desired permission levels.

    a. On the Review tab, in the Changes group, click Protect Sheet.

    b. If necessary, in the Password To Unprotect Sheet text box, type a password of your choice.

    c. In the Protect Sheet dialog box, in the Allow All Users Of This Worksheet To list box, check the tasks you want users to perform and click OK.

    d. If necessary, retype your password for confirmation and click OK.

    e. Click OK to close the Protect Sheet dialog box and save the settings.

Procedure Reference: Remove Specific Content from a Workbook

To remove specific content from a workbook by inspecting it:

1. Click the Office button and choose Prepare→Inspect Document.

2. If necessary, in the Microsoft Office Excel message box, click Yes to save the latest changes made to the workbook.

3. In the Document Inspector dialog box, check the check boxes corresponding to the content you want to inspect in the workbook and click Inspect.

4. Review the results displayed by the Document Inspector corresponding to the content you want to remove and click Remove All as needed.

5. If necessary, click Reinspect to inspect the workbook again.

6. Click Close.

Procedure Reference: Allow Users to Edit Specific Cell Ranges in a Password-Protected Worksheet

To allow users to edit specific cell ranges in a password-protected worksheet:

1. On the Review tab, in the Changes group, click Allow Users To Edit Ranges.

2. In the Allow Users To Edit Ranges dialog box, click New.

3. In the New Range dialog box, in the Title text box, type a title for the range.

4. Specify the range of cells that users can edit.
   - In the Refers To Cells text box, type the cell range.
   - Or, click the Range Selection button and select the desired range.

5. In the Range Password text box, type a password and click OK.

6. In the Confirm Password dialog box, retype the password for confirmation and click OK.

7. In the Allow Users To Edit Ranges dialog box, click Apply and then click OK.

Procedure Reference: Protect the Structure and Window Layout of Workbooks from Being Altered

To protect the structure and window layout of workbooks from being altered:

1. On the Review tab, in the Changes group, from the Protect Workbook drop-down list, select Protect Structure And Windows.

2. In the Protect Structure And Windows dialog box, in the Protect Workbook For section, specify the type of protection.
   - Check the Structure check box, to restrict users from adding, editing, or deleting worksheets.
   - Check the Windows check box, to ensure that the window always opens in the same size and position.

3. In the Password (Optional) text box, type a password to restrict access and then click OK.

4. Retype the password and click OK to confirm it.

Procedure Reference: Protect Workbooks from Being Opened or Modified

To protect workbooks from being opened:

1. Open the workbook you want to protect.

2. Click the Office button and choose Save As.

3. In the Save As dialog box, navigate to the folder in which you would like to save the file.

4. From the Tools menu, choose General Options.

5. In the General Options dialog box, in the File Sharing section, specify a password to open or modify a workbook.
   - In the Password To Open text box, type a password to open the file.
   - In the Password To Modify text box, type a password to modify the file.

6. Click OK.

7. In the Confirm Password dialog box, retype the password for confirmation and then click OK.

8. Click Save.

ACTIVITY 2-1

Protecting a Worksheet

Data Files:

Display.xlsx

Before You Begin:

From C:\084892Data\Collaborating with Others, open Display.xlsx.

Scenario:

The Display workbook contains a worksheet you want to give to other users. You have decided to allow anyone to open the file, select a cell or range of cells, and make formatting changes to the worksheet, but only someone with the worksheet's password can make changes to the numerical values stored in the worksheet.

What You Do	How You Do It
1. **Lock the contents in the worksheet and hide the formulas.**	a. **Select range A1:J11.**
	b. On the Home tab, in the Cells group, **click Format and select Format Cells.**
	c. In the Format Cells dialog box, **select the Protection tab.**
	d. **Check the Locked check box** to secure the data in the cells.
	e. **Check the Hidden check box** to hide the formulas in the cells.
	f. **Click OK.**

2.	**Password protect the worksheet allowing only selection of locked cells, unlocked cells, and formatting of cells.**	a. On the Review tab, in the Changes group, **click Protect Sheet.**
		b. In the Protect Sheet dialog box, in the Password To Unprotect Sheet text box, **type a7Q9x**
		c. In the Allow All Users Of This Worksheet To list box, **verify that the Select Locked Cells and Select Unlocked Cells check boxes are checked.**
		d. **Check the Format Cells check box and click OK.**
		e. In the Confirm Password dialog box, in the Reenter Password To Proceed text box, **type a7Q9x and click OK.**

3.	**Test your work.**	a. **Click cell B6.**
		b. Observe that the Formula bar remains blank and the cell content is hidden.
		c. **Double-click cell E5.**
		d. Observe that the Microsoft Office Excel warning box opens indicating that you are trying to change a protected cell. **Click OK.**
		e. **Select the cell range A5:A9.**
		f. On the Home tab, in the Font group, **click the Italic button** to italicize the sales people's names.

4.	**Check whether users with the password can edit the worksheet.**	a. On the Review tab, in the Changes group, **click Unprotect Sheet.**
		b. In the Unprotect Sheet dialog box, in the Password text box, **type a7Q9x and click OK.**
		c. **Click cell J3 and press Delete.**
		d. **Type 50 and press Enter** to change the value of the cell.
		e. **Save the workbook as My Display.xlsx**

ACTIVITY 2-2
Allowing Users to Edit a Specified Range

Before You Begin:

My Display.xlsx is open.

Scenario:

You have given your protected copy of display.xlsx to others. Some users would like to edit only the range of cells in the Bonus Table. You want to enable users to unlock the Bonus Table range with a password. The password for this range will differ from the password that allows users to unprotect the worksheet. Also, you want to check for any comments in the workbook and delete them in order to avoid confusion, as they are no longer valid.

What You Do	How You Do It
1. **Inspect the document for comments and remove them.**	a. In the worksheet, notice that there are comments in cells J8, I10, and I11, and then **click the Office button and choose Prepare→Inspect Document.**
	b. In the Document Inspector dialog box, **verify that the Comments And Annotations check box is checked.**

To check the document for the selected content, click Inspect.

☑ **Comments and Annotations**
　Inspects the document for comments and ink annotations.

	c. **Uncheck the other check boxes and click Inspect.**
	d. Observe the comments found in the document and **click Remove All** corresponding to the Comments And Annotations check box.
	e. Observe that the comments were successfully removed and **click Close.**

2. Define the entire range of cells in the Bonus Table as editable.

a. In the Changes group, **click Allow Users To Edit Ranges.**

b. In the Allow Users To Edit Ranges dialog box, **click New.**

c. In the New Range dialog box, in the Title text box, **type *Bonus Table* and press Tab** to move to the next text box.

d. In the Refers To Cells text box, **type *=I6:J11* and press Tab** to move to the next text box.

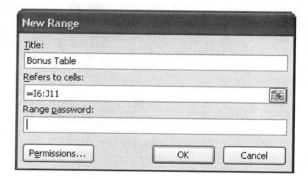

3. Assign a password to the range and then apply the protection.

a. In the Range Password text box, **type *7p9Ws* and click OK.**

b. In the Confirm Password dialog box, in the Reenter Password To Proceed text box, **type *7p9Ws* and click OK.**

c. In the Allow Users To Edit Ranges dialog box, **click Apply and then click OK.**

4. Protect the worksheet.

a. In the Changes group, **click Protect Sheet.**

b. In the Password To Unprotect Sheet text box, **type *a7Q9x***

c. In the Protect Sheet dialog box, **click OK.**

d. In the Confirm Password dialog box, **type *a7Q9x* and click OK.**

5. **Test your work.**

   a. **Double-click cell I8.**

   b. In the Unlock Range dialog box, in the Enter The Password To Change This Cell text box, **type *7p9Ws* and click OK.**

   c. **Type *45* and press Enter** to change the value of the cell.

   d. **Save the workbook as *My Display Range.xlsx* and close it.**

ACTIVITY 2-3

Protecting a Workbook

Data Files:

Regional Sales.xlsx

Before You Begin:

From C:\084892Data\Collaborating with Others, open Regional Sales.xlsx.

Scenario:

You have completed work on the Regional Sales workbook. Now you want to let others contribute to the workbook, but you don't want anyone to rearrange the worksheets or move the windows in the file. You also want to ensure that only users with the password can open the workbook.

What You Do	How You Do It
1. Password-protect the workbook's structure and windows.	a. On the Review tab, in the Changes group, **click Protect Workbook and select Protect Structure And Windows.**
	b. In the Protect Structure And Windows dialog box, observe that the Structure check box is checked by default.
	c. **Check the Windows check box** to ensure that the layout of the window always remains the same.
	d. In the Password (Optional) text box, **type *w2Tx7* and click OK.**
	e. In the Confirm Password dialog box, **type *w2Tx7* and click OK.**

2. **Try to modify the structure and window layout of the workbook.**

   a. **Drag the Southeast tab to the left** to test the structure of the workbook.

   b. On the View tab, in the Window group, **click Arrange All.**

   c. In the Arrange Windows dialog box, in the Arrange section, **select the Horizontal option and click OK** to test the window layout of the workbook.

   d. Observe that the window layout has not changed.

3. **Save the workbook with a password.**

   a. **Click the Office button and choose Save As.**

   b. In the Save As dialog box, from the Tools drop-down list, **select General Options.**

   c. In the General Options dialog box, in the Password To Open text box, **type *k610i* and click OK.**

   d. In the Confirm Password dialog box, **type *k610i* and click OK** to confirm the password.

   e. **Click Save.**

   f. In the Microsoft Office Excel warning box, **click Yes** to overwrite the file with the password protection.

   g. **Close the file.**

4. **Test the password-protected workbook.**

   a. **Open Regional Sales.xlsx.**

   b. In the Password dialog box, **type *k610i* and click OK.**

   c. **Close the file.**

TOPIC B

Share a Workbook

You have protected your workbook. Now you are ready to let others access it. In this topic, you will share a workbook.

You have created a complex workbook that many people in your organization will need to use. Before making the workbook live in your business environment, you decide to get some feedback on its design from the people who will be using it the most. Sharing workbooks makes it easy to create a single workbook that many people can access, manipulate, and respond to as necessary.

The SharePoint® Server

Microsoft® Office SharePoint® Server 2007 is a collaboration and content management server that is integrated with the Office 2007 suite. It acts as a repository of documents where files can be saved and accessed from different locations. The SharePoint server tracks the work done on a file by maintaining information on users and file versions. This server also acts as a common platform for hosting content from the Internet and an intranet. In addition, the SharePoint server can also be used to control access and content modification permissions for files stored on the server.

Shared Workbooks

Definition:

A *shared workbook* is a workbook which is set up and saved to allow multiple users on the same network to view, edit, and save the workbook at the same time. Each person who saves the shared workbook can see the changes that have been made by other users. A single portion of data can be changed by multiple users, and all the changes can be highlighted during review if the workbook is shared. When a workbook is shared, the text "Shared" appears on the title bar of the workbook.

 A shared workbook may not support certain Excel features such as deleting worksheets, merging cells, or splitting cells.

Example:

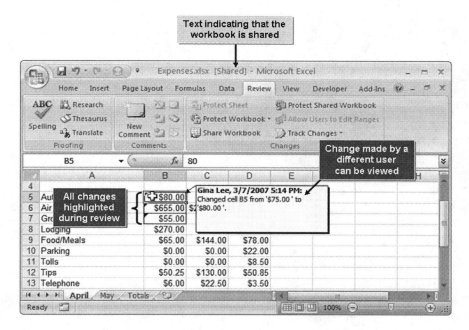

How to Share a Workbook

Procedure Reference: Share a Workbook

To share a workbook:

1. Open the file you want to share.

2. On the Review tab, in the Changes group, click Share Workbook.

3. In the Share Workbook dialog box, on the Editing tab, check the Allow Changes By More Than One User At The Same Time check box.

4. Set options on the Advanced tab.

   - Select options in the Track Changes section to display change history.

   - Select options in the Update Changes section to update the changes regularly.

   - Select options in the Conflicting Changes Between Users section to specify which changes to be retained.

   - Select options in the Include In Personal View section to specify print and filter settings.

5. Click OK.

6. In the Microsoft Office Excel warning box, click OK to save the workbook.

7. Click the Office button and choose Publish→Document Management Server.

8. In the Save As dialog box, select the shared network folder and click Open.

 The shared network folder has to be created manually in the My Network Places directory.

9. Select a location and click Save to save the document and to place the copy on the server.

DISCOVERY ACTIVITY 2-4

Creating a Shared Workbook

Data Files:

Create Shared Workbook_guided.exe

Simulation:

This is a simulated activity. In this simulation, SharePoint Server 2007 has been installed with the URL **http://adexchangesrv:34097**.

Scenario:

You are the human resources manager at your company. You need to share the phonelist file that contains the name, department, office, and phone extension information for employees. This is an informal list that each department manager will need to update periodically. Because each manager will need access to the file, you have decided to share the workbook and save it in a designated location on the network. You need to keep track of the changes made to the workbook in the last 15 days. You also realize that you need to add some more details of Jaco Prestia—a new human resources employee—to the Gwillis list that resides on the server. Jaco is in office 9f and his phone extension is 2699.

1. To launch the simulation, **browse to the C:\084892Data\Collaborating with Others\ Simulations folder.**

2. **Double-click the Create Shared Workbook_guided.exe file.**

3. **Maximize the simulation window.**

4. **Follow the on screen steps for the simulation.**

5. When you have finished the activity, **close the simulation window.**

TOPIC C
Set Revision Tracking

You shared data in workbooks. You want to set tracking options in order to track any changes made to a given worksheet or workbook. In this topic, you will set revision tracking.

You have a worksheet that other people in your organization will be manipulating. However, your business process dictates that you need to know who has made changes to the worksheet, when they made those changes, and what the changes were. By setting revision tracking, you can keep close track of who has made alterations to a given worksheet or workbook and what those alterations were.

Revision Tracking

Definition:

Revision tracking is a formatting technique used to track any change made to a workbook. Once a workbook is set to revision tracking mode, it becomes a shared workbook. Revision tracking is not a default option; it needs to be enabled for the changes to be highlighted. It tracks details such as the person who made the change, the date and time when the change was made, and where in the workbook the change was made.

Example:

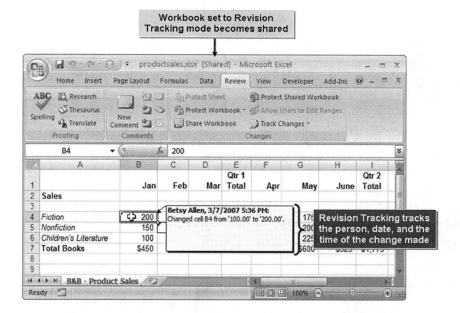

The Highlight Changes Dialog Box

The Highlight Changes dialog box is used to set highlighting options for revision tracking. This dialog box allows the user to enable track changing in the workbook. You can also set options to track changes based on who made the changes, when they were made, and where in the worksheet they were made.

How to Set Revision Tracking

Procedure Reference: Set Revision Tracking Using the Track Changes Command

To set revision tracking using the Track Changes command:

1. On the Review tab, in the Changes group, from the Track Changes drop-down list, select Highlight Changes to display the Highlight Changes dialog box.

2. Check the Track Changes While Editing check box to enable the track changes options.

3. In the Highlight Which Changes section, set the When, Who, and Where parameters as needed.

   - Check the When check box and select an option from the When drop-down list, to specify the period for which the changes need to be highlighted.

   - Check the Who check box and select an option from the Who drop-down list, to specify whose changes need to be highlighted.

   - Check the Where check box and enter the range of cells in the Where text box, for which the changes need to be highlighted.

4. Click OK.

5. In the message box that prompts you to save the changes in the workbook, click OK.

Procedure Reference: Set Revision Tracking Using the Protect And Share Workbook Command

To set revision tracking using the Protect And Share Workbook command:

1. On the Review tab, in the Changes group, click Protect And Share Workbook.

2. In the Protect Shared Workbook dialog box, check the Sharing With Track Changes check box and click OK.

3. In the confirmation dialog box, click OK.

Procedure Reference: Display All the Changes Made to the Workbook

To display all the changes made to the workbook:

1. Open the file with changes made to it.

2. From the Track Changes drop-down list, select Highlight Changes.

3. In the Highlight Changes dialog box, uncheck the When, Who, and Where check boxes in order to view all the changes.

4. If necessary, on cells that have a small triangle in the top-left corner, hover your mouse pointer to view the revision note made by the user.

ACTIVITY 2-5
Setting Revision Tracking

Data Files:

Product Sales_01.xlsx, Product Sales_02.xlsx

Before You Begin:

From C:\084892Data\Collaborating with Others, open Product Sales_01.xlsx.

Scenario:

You have entered the necessary details into the Product Sales_01 workbook. Another person in your organization will need to add more music genres to the CDs And Tapes section of the workbook. You need to set the options in order to track every change made to the file so that you can validate the new data.

You have one more workbook that has to be sent to the Sales Manager for review. You decide to enable the option for viewing the changes made by the Manager so that you can later accept or reject them.

What You Do	How You Do It
1. Turn on revision tracking in the Product Sales_01 workbook using the Track Changes command.	a. On the Review tab, in the Changes group, **click Track Changes and select Highlight Changes.**
	b. In the Highlight Changes dialog box, **check the Track Changes While Editing check box.**
	c. In the Highlight Which Changes section, **check the Who check box,** observe that the Everyone option is selected from the Who drop-down list, and **click OK.**
	d. In the Microsoft Office Excel message box, **click OK** to save the changes to the workbook.
2. Test your work.	a. **Right-click cell A4 and choose Insert.**
	b. In the Insert dialog box, **click OK** to insert a new row.

c. **Hover the mouse pointer over the tri-angle in the top-left corner of cell A4** and observe that a comment box appears with the revision note you made.

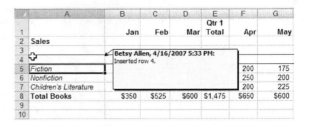

d. **Save and close the file.**

---

3. **Set review tracking in Product Sales_02 using the Protect And Share Workbook command.**

a. **Open C:\084892Data\Collaborating with Others, and open Product Sales_ 02.xlsx.**

b. On the Review tab, in the Changes group, **click Protect And Share Workbook.**

c. In the Protect Shared Workbook dialog box, **check the Sharing With Track Changes check box and click OK.**

d. In the Microsoft Office Excel message box, **click OK** to save the changes to the workbook.

e. **Close the file.**

TOPIC D
Review Tracked Revisions

You have set revision tracking for your files. You now want to see what changes have been made to the file, and to accept or reject them as required. In this topic, you will review tracked revisions.

You created a workbook, set revision tracking and then sent the workbook out for review. You have now received the workbook back from one of your colleagues, and are in the process of verifying whether or not any of the changes he made are viable. By reviewing tracked revisions, you can sure that any revisions made to a file are correct before the core content of the file is changed.

The Accept/Reject Changes Option

The Accept/Reject Changes option from the Track Changes drop-down list of the Changes group allows you to decide which changes you want to retain and which to discard after a tracked review. Selecting this option displays the Select Changes To Accept Or Reject dialog box. Options regarding which changes to be selected, such as when the changes were made, who made the changes, and where the changes were made in the workbook, can be set using the dialog box. When you click OK, the Accept Or Reject Changes dialog box is displayed with the details of the changes made to the workbook. It also has options to accept or reject the changes.

How to Review Tracked Revisions
Procedure Reference: Accept or Reject Tracked Changes

To accept or reject tracked changes:

1. On the Review tab, in the Changes group, from the Track Changes drop-down list, select Accept/Reject Changes.
2. In the Select Changes To Accept Or Reject dialog box, identify what changes you want to make.
   - In the Which Changes section, select When to display the changes by specifying when the changes were made.
   - In the Which Changes section, select Who to display the changes by specifying who made the changes.
   - In the Which Changes section, select Where to display the changes by specifying the range of cells in which the changes were made.
3. Click OK.
4. In the Accept Or Reject Changes dialog box, accept or reject changes as needed.
   - Click Accept to accept a single change.
   - Click Accept All to accept all changes.
   - Click Reject to reject a single change.
   - Click Reject All to reject all changes.

ACTIVITY 2-6
Accepting and Rejecting Tracked Changes

Data Files:

Reviewed Product Sales.xlsx

Before You Begin:

From C:\084892Data\Collaborating with Others, open Reviewed Product Sales.xlsx.

Scenario:

You just received the product sales workbook back, and you are ready to review the changes made to the file. The details for the Hip-hop music sales have been modified. You need to list the changes on a new worksheet, highlight the changes on-screen, and accept or reject them as needed.

What You Do	How You Do It
1. Highlight the changes made by Esme, and list the changes on a new worksheet.	a. On the Review tab, in the Changes group, **click Track Changes and select Highlight Changes.**
	b. In the Highlight Changes dialog box, from the When drop-down list, **select All.**
	c. **Check the Who check box,** and from the Who drop-down list, **select Esme.**
	d. **Check the List Changes On A New Sheet check box and click OK** to list the changes in a new History worksheet.
2. Accept the changes in the B&B - Product Sales worksheet.	a. **Select the B&B - Product Sales worksheet tab.**
	b. In the Changes group, **click Track Changes and select Accept/Reject Changes** to open the Select Changes To Accept Or Reject dialog box.
	c. Observe the default settings and **click OK.**

d. In the Accept Or Reject Changes dialog box, observe that the value has been changed from 165.00 to 164.00.

e. **Click Accept** to accept the first change, and observe that the next change is highlighted.

f. **Click Accept repeatedly until all the changes are accepted.**

g. **Save the file as *My Reviewed Product Sales.xlsx* and close it.**

TOPIC E
Merge Workbooks

You have reviewed tracked changes in your workbook. Now you have multiple related workbooks, and you would like to consolidate them into a single workbook. In this topic, you will merge workbooks.

You have individual sales data worksheets for the last 12 fiscal quarters. The vice-president of sales has called and wants to run some numbers on all of that data. Rather than send the VP 12 separate files, you decide to consolidate them into a single file. Merging workbooks helps organize related data into one file.

The Compare and Merge Workbooks Option

The Compare And Merge Workbooks option allows the user to merge multiple copies of a shared workbook. This option does not appear on the Ribbon by default, and it needs to be added to the Quick Access toolbar by using the Excel Options dialog box. The Compare And Merge Workbooks command is activated only if the workbook is shared. The shared workbook that will contain the merge—and all of the other workbooks you want to merge into it—must be copies of the same shared workbook.

How to Merge Workbooks

Procedure Reference: Display the Compare And Merge Workbooks Option on the Quick Access Toolbar

To display the Compare And Merge Workbooks option on the Quick Access toolbar:

1.   Click the Office button and then click Excel Options.
2.   In the Excel Options dialog box, in the Customize category, from the Choose Commands From drop-down list, select All Commands.
3.   In the All Commands list box, select Compare And Merge Workbooks and click Add.
4.   Click OK to close the dialog box and to add the button to the Quick Access toolbar.

Procedure Reference: Merge Workbooks

To merge workbooks:

1.   Save the different copies of the shared workbook in a folder along with the main copy.
2.   Open the workbook into which you would like other workbooks to merge.
3.   On the Quick Access toolbar, click the Compare And Merge Workbooks button.
4.   In the Select Files To Merge Into Current Workbook dialog box, navigate to your folder and select the file(s) you would like to merge into the open workbook.
5.   Click OK to merge the workbooks.

ACTIVITY 2-7
Merging Workbooks

Data Files:

Personnel Human Resources.xlsx, Personnel Accounting.xlsx, Personnel Customer Service.xlsx, Personnel Development.xlsx, Personnel Engineering.xlsx, Personnel Tech Support.xlsx

Before You Begin:

From C:\084892Data\Collaborating with Others, open Personnel Human Resources.xlsx.

Scenario:

You have created and shared an Excel workbook named Personnel Human Resources that acts as a contact list for employees. You have asked the managers of the accounting, customer service, development, engineering, and technical support departments to review the contact list information for their respective departments. All of the managers have updated the file as needed and then renamed their version of the file with their department name. You now want to make one file out of all of the separate department files.

What You Do	How You Do It
1. Display the Compare And Merge button on the Quick Access toolbar.	a. **Click the Office button and then click Excel Options.**
	b. In the Excel Options dialog box, in the Customize category, from the Choose Commands From drop-down list, **select All Commands.**
	c. In the All Commands list box, **scroll down, select Compare And Merge Workbooks, and click Add.**
	d. **Click OK** to close the dialog box and to add the button to the Quick Access toolbar.

2. **Merge the contents of the files from each department with the Personnel Human Resources workbook.**

a. On the Quick Access toolbar, **click the Compare And Merge Workbooks button.**

b. In the Select Files To Merge Into Current Workbook dialog box, **select the Personnel Accounting.xlsx, Personnel Customer Service.xlsx, Personnel Development.xlsx, Personnel Engineering.xlsx, and Personnel Tech Support.xlsx files.**

c. **Click OK** to close the dialog box and to merge the files.

d. **Save the file as *My Personnel Human Resources.xlsx* and close it.**

TOPIC F

Administer Digital Signatures

You have adjusted macro settings for a workbook in Excel. Workbooks with macros are sensitive files. You might need to share the files with others, and people who receive your files need to verify that you are the originator of the files you send. In this topic, you will administer digital signatures.

You have been receiving a large number of expense reports from a particular salesperson. When you call her, she denies ever sending the reports in question. You ask her to attach a digital signature to all of her future reports so that you can verify that they are coming from her. Digital signatures add an extra level of security to shared files by confirming the identity of the person who originated the files.

Digital Certificates

Definition:

A *digital certificate* is an electronic file that contains unique information about a specific person. It contains a serial number, the digital signature of the certificate-issuing authority, expiration dates, a name, and a copy of the certificate holder's public key so that a recipient can verify that the certificate is authentic. It is issued by a certification authority (CA), which is a trusted third party, or from your own company's computer service professional. A digital certificate is also known as a digital ID as it is used to digitally sign a document.

Example:

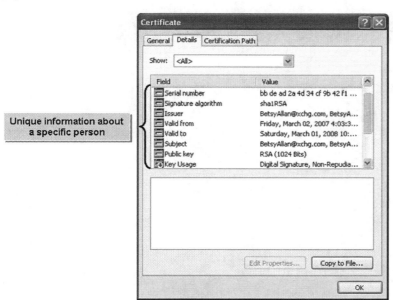

Digital Signatures

Definition:

A *digital signature* is a content authentication tool that authenticates the originator of a file, and ensures the integrity of digital documents. It validates the authenticity, integrity, and origin of the document. The digital signature is not visible within the contents of the workbook. The Signature icon on the Microsoft Office Status Bar at the bottom of the application window is indicative of the fact that the workbook has been digitally signed. When you open a document with a digital signature, the details will be visible in the Signatures pane of your workbook. Users cannot make modifications to a digitally signed document until the signature is removed.

Example:

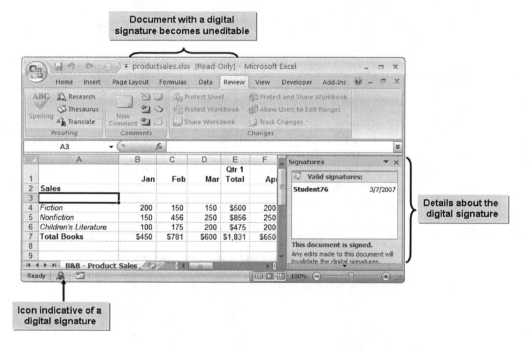

How to Administer Digital Signatures

Procedure Reference: Add a Digital Signature to a File

To add a digital signature to a file:

1. Click the Office button and choose Prepare→Add A Digital Signature.

2. In the Microsoft Office Excel dialog box, click OK.

3. If necessary, create a digital ID.

    a. In the Get A Digital ID dialog box, select Create Your Own Digital ID.

 The Get A Digital ID dialog box appears only if you attempt to digitally sign a document without a digital certificate.

    b. In the Create A Digital ID dialog box, type the necessary information.

        1. In the Name text box, type a name.

        2. In the E-mail Address text box, type an email address.

        3. In the Organization text box, type the name of an organization or company.

        4. In the Location text box, type the geographic location.

4. In the Sign dialog box, in the Purpose For Signing This Document text box, enter the purpose in adding the digital signature.

5. If necessary, change the digital certificate.

    a. In the Signing As section, click Change.

    b. In the Select Certificate dialog box, select the desired certificate and click OK.

6. Click Sign.

7. In the Signature Confirmation message box, click OK.

8. In the Signatures pane, view the digital signature and the certificate icon on the Microsoft Office Status Bar.

Procedure Reference: Install Another Person's Certificate on Your Computer

To install another person's certificate on your computer:

1. In the Security Warning panel below the Ribbon, click Options.

2. If necessary, under File Sharing Settings For This Workbook, click Digital Signatures.

3. In the Microsoft Office Security Options dialog box, in the Signature section, click the Show Signature Details link.

4. In the Digital Signature Details dialog box, on the General tab, click View Certificate.

5. In the Certificate dialog box, click Install Certificate.

6. In the Certificate Import Wizard screen, click Next.

7. On the Certificate Store page, select the desired storage location.

    • Select Automatically Select The Certificate Store Based On The Type Of Certificate.

    • Select Place All Certificates In The Following Store to select the desired location.

        a. Click Browse and choose the desired location.

        b. In the Select Certificate Store dialog box, select the certificate store you want to use and click OK.

8. Click Next.

9. Click Finish, and then in the dialog box that confirms a successful import, click OK.

10. In the Certificate dialog box, click OK.

11. In the Digital Signature Details dialog box, click OK.

12. In the Microsoft Office Security Options dialog box, select Trust All Documents From This Publisher and click OK to add the source as a trusted publisher.

Procedure Reference: Remove a Digital Signature from a File

To remove a digital signature from a file:

1. Open a file that has been digitally signed.

2. View the digital signature in the file.

   - Click the Office button and choose Prepare→View Signatures.

   - Or, on the panel below the Ribbon, click View Signatures.

3. Remove the signature.

   - In the Signatures pane, place the mouse pointer over the signature, click the drop-down arrow, and select Remove Signature.

   - Or, right-click the signature and choose Remove Signature.

4. In the Remove Signature dialog box, click Yes.

5. In the Signature Removed message box, click OK.

ACTIVITY 2-8

Administering Digital Signatures

Data Files:

Employee Contact Info.xlsx, Allan.xlsm

Before You Begin:

From C:\084892Data\Collaborating with Others, open Employee Contact Info.xlsx.

Verify the macro setting is set to disable all macros with notification.

Scenario:

Your company has assigned you a digital ID. With it, you need to digitally sign the employee contact information document, so that when your manager requests the file, she can confirm that it came from you.

The second thing she needs you to do is open the Allan workbook and install Betsy Allan's certificate on your computer, because you will regularly be corresponding with her.

What You Do	How You Do It
1. Digitally sign the file.	a. Save the file as *My Employee Contact Info.xlsx*
	b. **Click the Office button and choose Prepare→Add A Digital Signature.**
	c. In the Microsoft Office Excel dialog box, **click OK.**
	d. In the Sign dialog box, in the Purpose For Signing This Document text box, **type *Confidential* and click Sign.**
	e. In the Signature Confirmation message box, **click OK.**
	f. Observe that the certificate icon ![icon] appears on the Microsoft Office Status Bar, and the signature owner's name is displayed in the Signatures pane.
2. **Install the digital certificate in the Allan workbook to your Trusted Root Certification Authorities store.**	a. **Open Allan.xlsm.**
	b. In the Security Warning panel, **click Options.**

c. In the Microsoft Office Security Options dialog box, in the Signature section, observe that the file has been digitally signed by Betsy Allan.

> Signature
>
> Signed by: BetsyAllan
> Certificate expiration: 3/1/2008
> Certificate issued by: BetsyAllan
> Show Signature Details

> ⊛ Help protect me from unknown content (recommended)

d. In the Signature section, **click the Show Signature Details link.**

e. In the Digital Signature Details dialog box, on the General tab, **click View Certificate.**

f. In the Certificate dialog box, **click Install Certificate.**

g. In the Certificate Import Wizard screen, **click Next.**

h. On the Certificate Store page, **select the Place All Certificates In The Following Store option and click Browse.**

i. In the Select Certificate Store dialog box, **select the Trusted Root Certification Authorities store and click OK.**

j. On the Certificate Store page, **click Next.**

k. On the Completing the Certificate Import Wizard page, **click Finish.**

l. If necessary, in the Security Warning box, **click Yes.**

m. In the message box that confirms a successful import, **click OK.**

n. In the Certificate dialog box, **click OK.**

o. In the Digital Signature Details dialog box, **click OK.**

p. In the Microsoft Office Security Options dialog box, **select the Trust All Documents From This Publisher option and click OK.**

3. **View Betsy Allan's digital certificate installed on your computer.**

a. **Open the Excel Options dialog box.**

b. **Select the Trust Center category,** and in the right pane, **click Trust Center Settings.**

c. In the Trust Center dialog box, **select the Trusted Publishers category,** and in the right pane, **select BetsyAllan.**

d. **Click View,** and in the Certificate dialog box, observe the certificate information.

e. **Click OK** to close the Certificate dialog box.

f. **Click OK** to close the Trust Center dialog box.

g. **Close the Excel Options dialog box.**

h. **Close all open files and the Signatures task pane.**

TOPIC G
Restrict Document Access

Digital signatures guarantee that files are from who they say they are from. But you will also want to ensure the file has not been modified, either accidentally or on purpose.

When you are creating a workbook by yourself, there is no need to worry about the security of its contents. But when you circulate it within a team, you will have to prevent unnecessary modification of the content. By restricting document permissions, you can ensure that the workbook is modified only by people to whom you assign permissions.

Information Rights Management

Information Rights Management (IRM) is a service that permits users and administrators to define permissions for users to access presentations, documents, and workbooks, as well as other Office suite application documents such as Outlook and Microsoft Access. The permissions assigned to a file are stored with the file's content. All data present within a document is bound by these permissions. The IRM also enables you to prohibit the printing, forwarding, or copying of sensitive data. The content also cannot be copied using the Print Screen mode of Windows. In addition, you can set an expiration date to restrict file access after a specific time frame. IRM is otherwise known as DRM (Digital Rights Management).

Windows Rights Management Services Client with Service Pack 2

If you are using Windows XP as the operating system for your computer, the Windows Rights Management Services Client with Service Pack 2, which is the IRM administrator, needs to be installed. The Rights Management account certificate becomes available on your system upon installation of the Windows Rights Management Services Client with Service Pack 2. Organization-specific policies on copying, forwarding, and editing can be configured using the server.

The Rights Management Account Certificate

For those who are not using the IRM administrator, there is an option for using your email address and password configured on .NET Passport, MSN, or Hotmail. Your email address is used to create the Rights Management account certificate that is downloaded to your computer. You can choose to download a standard certificate or a temporary certificate, depending on use. Once the Rights Management account certificate is downloaded, you can create user accounts, which is the addition of the email address of the persons to whom you will send your workbook. You can give the users full control over your workbook or restrict the users to read, print, or copy.

Standard and Temporary Certificates

You can choose to download a standard certificate or a temporary certificate when you are using your email address and password to download the Rights Management account certificate. If you are going to use the content in the workbook for a limited time, or if you are using a public computer to send your workbook, then the temporary certificate will suffice. Downloading the standard certificate enables you to create, use, and view restricted content on your PC. The certificate can also be renewed on its expiration.

The Mark As Final Command

The *Mark As Final* command enables you to certify a document as final, and protect it from further modifications. After marking a workbook final, all editing commands are disabled, and the workbook goes into a read-only mode. The status is displayed as Final in the Document Information panel, and the Mark As Final icon is displayed on the Microsoft Office Status Bar.

How to Restrict Document Access

Procedure Reference: Restrict Permission to Contents in a File

To restrict permission to contents in a file:

1. Display the Select User dialog box.
    - Click the Office button and choose Prepare→Restrict Permission→Manage Credentials.
    - Or, on the Review tab, in the Changes group, from the Protect Workbook drop-down list, select Manage Credentials.
2. In the Select User dialog box, select your user name and click OK.
3. In the Permission dialog box, check the Restrict Permission To This Workbook check box.
4. Restrict permissions to users.
    - Grant read permission to users.
        - In the Read text box, type the email address of the user to whom you want to grant read-only rights.
        - Or, click Read, and in the Select Users Or Groups dialog box, enter the email address of the user to whom you want to grant read-only rights.
    - Grant change permission to users.
        - In the Change text box, type the email address of the user to whom you want to grant editing rights.
        - Or, click Change, and in the Select Users Or Groups dialog box, enter the email address of the user to whom you want to grant editing rights.
5. In the Permission dialog box, click OK.
6. If desired, click More Options and set additional options.
7. If necessary, save the workbook.

Permission Levels

The three levels of permission allowed are read, change, and full control. However, you can change the permission levels given to a user depending on the requirements.

Level of Permission	*Description*
Read	Allows users to only read the document. They cannot edit, copy, or print it.
Change	Allows users to read, edit, and save changes to the document; however, they cannot print it.
Full Control	Allows users to own full control of the document.

Procedure Reference: Set an Expiration Date for a File

To set an expiration date for a file:

1. If necessary, open the file.
2. Click the Office button and choose Prepare→Restrict Permission→Manage Credentials.
3. In the Select User dialog box, select your user name and click OK.
4. In the Permission dialog box, check the Restrict Permission To This Workbook check box.
5. Click More Options.
6. Under Additional Permissions For Users, check the This Workbook Expires On check box.
7. Select a date from the drop-down list or type a new date to specify the expiration date for the file and click OK.

Procedure Reference: View a Permission-Restricted Workbook

To view a permission-restricted workbook:

1. Open a workbook that is permission-restricted.
2. In the Microsoft Excel message box that states that permission is restricted to the worksheet, click OK.
3. On the message bar, click View Permission.
4. In the My Permission dialog box, note the permissions you have and click OK.
5. In you have the correct rights, make any desired changes to the workbook and save it.

Procedure Reference: Mark a Workbook as Final

To mark a workbook as final:

1. Open an existing workbook.
2. Click the Office button and choose Prepare→Mark As Final.
3. In the Microsoft Office Excel warning box, click OK to mark the workbook as final, and save the file.
4. In the Microsoft Office Excel information box, click OK.

DISCOVERY ACTIVITY 2-9
Restricting Document Access

Data Files:

Restrict Access_guided.exe

Simulation:

This is a simulated activity. In this simulation, you are Student 75 and your email address is student75@xchg.com. The Microsoft Right Management Service is available on your network.

Scenario:

You have a workbook that contains the quarterly sales data of the financial year. You want to send it to the finance manager, Betsy Allen, for review, and in case she has any edits to make, you also want to grant her permission to do so. Since this is confidential information, sharing the file could lead to some unnecessary tampering by external sources; therefore, you want to set permission in a manner that only the financial manager can edit the document. You also want to set an expiration date for the document so that the document cannot be accessed or opened after a certain period of time.

1. To launch the simulation, **browse to the C:\084892Data\Collaborating with Others\ Simulations folder.**

2. **Double-click the Restrict Access_guided.exe file.**

3. **Maximize the simulation window.**

4. **Follow the on screen steps for the simulation.**

5. When you have finished the activity, **close the simulation window.**

DISCOVERY ACTIVITY 2-10

Viewing a Permission-Restricted Workbook

Data Files:

View Permission Restricted Workbook_guided.exe

Simulation:

This is a simulated activity. In this simulation you have logged on to the company domain as Betsy Allan and your email address is betsyallan@xchg.com.

Scenario:

You have received quarterly sales data from one of your team members. You verify that you have change permission to the workbook. You review it and notice that the Jazz music sales data for March is incorrect. Therefore, you make the necessary change and save the document.

---

1. To launch the simulation, **browse to the C:\084892Data\Collaborating with Others\ Simulations folder.**

---

2. **Double-click the View Permission Restricted Workbook_guided.exe file.**

---

3. **Maximize the simulation window.**

---

4. **Follow the on screen steps for the simulation.**

---

5. When you have finished the activity, **close the simulation window.**

ACTIVITY 2-11

Marking a Workbook as Final

Data Files:

Final.xlsx

Before You Begin:

From C:\084892Data\Collaborating with Others, open Final.xlsx.

Scenario:

You have created a workbook, incorporated the necessary changes, and had it approved by your manager. Before sending it to your client, you want to share it with your colleague, but do not want her to make any changes to it.

What You Do	How You Do It
1. Mark the workbook as final.	a. Save the file as *My Final.xlsx*
	b. **Click the Office button and choose Prepare→Mark As Final.**
	c. In the Microsoft Office Excel warning box, **click OK** to mark the workbook as final and to save the file.
	d. In the Microsoft Office Excel message box indicating that the document is the final version, **click OK.**
	e. **Close the workbook.**
2. Verify that the workbook has been marked as final.	a. **Open My Final.xlsx.**
	b. **Click the Office button and place the mouse pointer over Prepare.**

c. Observe that the Mark As Final command is highlighted in the menu indicating that the file has been marked as final.

d. **Click anywhere in the workbook** to deselect the Office button menu.

e. **Close the workbook.**

Lesson 2 Follow-up

In this lesson, you took a number of actions that facilitate collaborating with others.

1.   **What projects are you currently working on that would benefit from collaboration with other people in your organization? How would you incorporate collaboration into the development process?**

2.   **What information do you think you will want to protect the most in your workbooks before you share them?**

3 | Auditing Worksheets

Lesson Time: 1 hour(s)

Lesson Objectives:

In this lesson, you will audit worksheets.

You will:

- Trace precedents and dependents of a cell.
- Troubleshoot errors in formulas.
- Troubleshoot invalid data and formulas.
- Watch and evaluate formulas.
- Create a data list outline.

Introduction

You have worksheets with data you need to interpret. Before interpreting the data, you need to verify that the data and formulas in your worksheets are accurate. In this lesson, you will audit worksheets.

You have a worksheet that has data with complex formulas and is error-riddled. The data should be verified and checked for errors, so it functions properly and provides you with the output you need. By auditing worksheets you can verify data validity and ensure that formulas, functions, and data all work together in the way you intended.

TOPIC A

Trace Cells

Have you ever experienced this: You know your data is incorrect, but you cannot determine what the problem is. You now need to troubleshoot a formula that is not providing you with the results you expected. In this topic, you will trace cell precedents and dependents.

You have a worksheet that contains complex formulas. However, the formula isn't producing the results you expected. After running a detailed analysis, you realize that the formula is referring to cell C97 when it should be referring to cell D97. Furthermore, you know that the Tax value stored in cell D15 is used in some of these formulas, but you are not sure which formulas correspond to the value in cell D15, or where the formulas are located in the worksheet. Tracing precedents and dependents of a cell helps verify the validity of a given formula and makes it easier to locate formulas in large worksheets when you know where the data in the formula is located, but not where the formula itself is located.

Tracer Arrows

Definition:

Tracer arrows are graphic illustrations depicting data flow between cells that contain values and those that contain formulas. These arrows point in the direction that your data flows. There are three types of tracer arrows: formula tracer arrows that appear as solid blue, error tracer arrows that appear as solid red, and external reference tracer arrows that appear as dashed black arrows preceded by a worksheet icon.

Example:

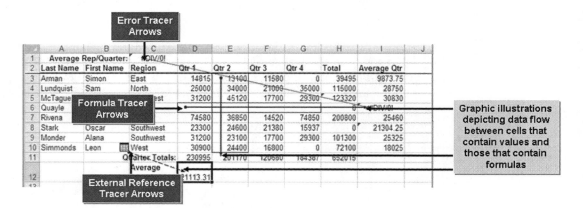

Cell Precedents

Definition:

A *cell precedent* is a cell reference in a formula that supplies data to the formula. It shows arrows to indicate the cells from where the data is fetched for the formula. In Excel, the Trace Precedents button is used to check formulas and to graphically display or trace the relationship between cells and formulas using arrows.

Example:

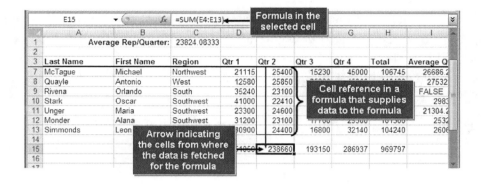

Cell Dependents

Definition:

A *cell dependent* is a cell that contains a formula referring to other cells. It displays arrows to indicate the cells that are affected by the value of the currently selected cell. The cell that contains the formula should not be included in the formula, and it should have a direct connection to the dependent cell. The dependent cell is highlighted by either red or blue arrows depending on the error in the cell.

Example:

The figure depicts the cell dependents for the selected cell.

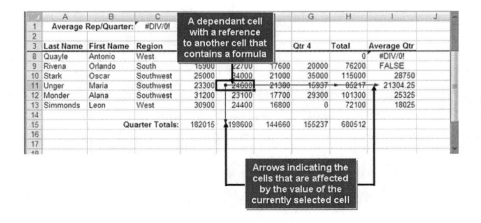

How to Trace Precedents and Dependents of a Cell

Procedure Reference: Trace Cell Precedents and Cell Dependents

To trace cell precedents and cell dependents:

1. In the worksheet, select the cell that contains the formula or data for which you want to trace precedent cells of dependent cells.

2. On the Formulas tab, in the Formula Auditing group, click Trace Precedents or Trace Dependents to trace the desired cells.

3. If necessary, double-click the tip of the tracer arrow to select the related cell or cell range.

4. If necessary, click Trace Precedents or Trace Dependents again to identify the next level of cells that provide data to the active cell.

5. In the Formula Auditing group, from the Remove Arrows drop-down list, select the necessary options in order to remove the arrows.

ACTIVITY 3-1

Tracing Precedents and Dependents of a Cell

Data Files:

Auditing.xlsx

Before You Begin:

From C:\084892Data\Auditing Worksheets, open Auditing.xlsx.

Scenario:

In your Auditing workbook, you have entered the details on the first quarter sales. Since this file will be distributed to a number of people, you want to make sure that the cell references used in the formula to calculate the first quarter sales as well as the grand total sales of all the quarters are correct. On completion of that, you need to display arrows that indicate what cells are affected by the value of the cell corresponding to Alana Monder's quarter 1 sales. You also need to view all relationships for the cell in the worksheet and identify the next level of cells that provide data to the active cell.

What You Do	How You Do It
1. In the Auditing workbook, **trace the precedents for the first quarter total sales.**	a. **Click cell D15.**
	b. On the Formulas tab, in the Formula Auditing group, **click Trace Precedents.**
	c. Observe that Excel draws a blue box around the range of cells to which the formula refers, and also draws a tracer arrow from the first cell in the precedent range, through the entire precedent range, and to the active cell.

	A	B	C	D	E	F
1		Average Rep/Quarter:	#DIV/0!			
2						
3	Last Name	First Name	Region	Qtr 1	Qtr 2	Qtr 3
6	Lundquist	Sam	North	25000	34000	21000
7	McTague	Michael	Northwest	0	0	0
8	Quayle	Antonio	West			
9	Rivena	Orlando	South			
10	Stark	Oscar	Southwest			
11	Unger	Maria	Southwest	23300	24600	21380
12	Monder	Alana	Southwest	31200	23100	17700
13	Simmonds	Leon	West	30900	24400	16800
14						
15			Quarter Totals:	141115	141900	106060

d. **Double-click the tip of the tracer arrow** to select the entire precedent range.

e. Observe that the range selected to calculate the first quarter total sales is correct.

| 2. | Remove the precedent arrows. | a. | **Click cell D15.** |
| | | b. | In the Formula Auditing group, **click the Remove Arrows button drop-down arrow and select Remove Precedent Arrows** to remove the precedent arrows. |

3.	Display two levels of precedent arrows for cell H15 and then remove all the arrows.	a.	**Click cell H15.**
		b.	In the Formula Auditing group, **click the Trace Precedents button** to view the precedent arrows.
		c.	**Click the Trace Precedents button again** to view two levels of precedent arrows.
		d.	**Click the Remove Arrows button.**

4.	Trace all of the dependents for Alana Monder's quarter 1 sales.	a.	**Click cell D12** to select Alana Monder's first quarter sales.
		b.	In the Formula Auditing group, **click Trace Dependents** to display the dependent tracer arrows.
		c.	Observe that cell D12 has dependence to total and average sales of all the quarters for Alana Monder and also has dependence to the quarter 1 totals.
		d.	**Click Trace Dependents** to display the next level of dependent tracer arrows and view all relationships in the cell.
		e.	Observe that there is a second level of dependence to the grand totals of all the quarters, and to the average of all average sales per quarter.

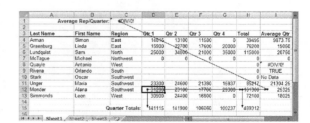

5. **Remove all dependent arrows.**

    a. In the Formula Auditing group, **click the Remove Arrows button drop-down arrow and select Remove Dependent Arrows** to remove the dependent arrows.

    b. From the Remove Arrows drop-down list, **select Remove Dependent Arrows** to remove the next level of dependent arrows.

    c. **Close the file without saving changes.**

TOPIC B
Troubleshoot Errors in Formulas

You have used cell precedents and cell dependents to verify data results in a formula. You now have a formula that does not display the expected result. In this topic, you will locate errors in formulas and fix them.

Do you want to use a worksheet that doesn't work because it has error-riddled formulas? Troubleshooting errors in formulas helps you quickly locate and fix problems in formulas so that they can function properly and provide you with the data you need.

The Error Checking Command

The *Error Checking* command on the Formula Auditing group of the Formula tab has options to check for errors in a formula. By using these options, errors in a formula cab be detected by the display of an icon next to the cell with the error and the appearance of colored arrows to trace the root of the error.

Error Types

There are a number of errors you may encounter displayed in a worksheet. Each type of error has a different cause. All formula errors begin with a pound sign (#).

Error Type	Description
#DIV/0!	Occurs when the numerical value in a cell is divided by 0.
#N/A	Occurs when a function or formula does not have a value.
#NAME?	Occurs when text is not recognized in a formula.
#NULL!	Occurs when you specify an intersection for values that cannot be intersected.
#NUM!	Occurs when there are invalid numeric values in a formula.
#REF!	Occurs when the reference to a cell is considered invalid.
#VALUE!	Occurs when an improper type of argument is used.
#####	Occurs when the cell contains a number, date, or time that is wider than the cell, or when the cell contains a date and/or time formula that produces a negative result.

How to Troubleshoot Errors in Formulas

Procedure Reference: Troubleshoot Errors in Formulas

To troubleshoot errors in formulas:

1. Click the cell that contains the formula with the error.
2. On the Formulas tab, in the Formula Auditing group, from the Error Checking drop-down list, select Trace Error to trace the errors in the file.
3. If desired, remove all trace arrows.
4. Fix the errors in the formula.
5. If necessary, trace more errors and fix them.
6. Save and close the file.

ACTIVITY 3-2
Troubleshooting Errors in Formulas

Data Files:

Auditing Error.xlsx

Before You Begin:

From C:\084892Data\Auditing Worksheets, open Auditing Error.xlsx.

Scenario:

In the Auditing Error workbook, the formula that you have used to calculate the average sales made by each of the sales executives for the second quarter is not displaying the correct values. You need to locate the error and fix it.

What You Do	How You Do It
1. Trace the error in the average sales per person for the second quarter.	a. **Click cell E18.**
	b. Observe that the Error Checking icon ⬦ appears next to the cell indicating an error in the cell.
	c. On the Formulas tab, in the Formula Auditing group, **click the Error Checking button drop-down arrow and select Trace Error** to trace the error in the selected cell.
	d. On the Formula bar, observe that you have entered the formula as =AVG(E4+E13) instead of =AVERAGE(E4:E13) in cell E18.
2. Make corrections to the formula.	a. In the Formula Auditing group, **click Remove Arrows** to remove the trace arrows.
	b. In the Formula bar, **select the formula.**
	c. **Type =AVERAGE(E4:E13) and press Enter.**

3. **Test your work.**

    a. **Click cell E18.**

    b. In the Formula Auditing group, **click the Error Checking button drop-down arrow and select Trace Error** to test for errors.

    c. Observe that the Trace Error command does not locate any error in the active cell, and in the Microsoft Office Excel warning box, **click OK.**

    d. **Save the file as *My Auditing Error.xlsx* and close it.**

TOPIC C
Troubleshoot Invalid Data and Formulas

You have fixed errors in formulas. To make optimal use of the data in the worksheet, you not only need to fix errors in the formulas, but also ensure that the worksheet does not contain invalid information. In this topic, you will troubleshoot invalid data and formulas.

Your Quarterly Sales worksheet contains invalid information in some of its formulas and data. You need to get this file to your manager so that she can make some critical business decisions at tomorrow morning's meeting with the VP of sales. Locating invalid data and formulas helps keep your data accurate by pointing out the invalid data so that you can fix it.

Invalid Data

Invalid data is any data in a cell that does not conform to the cell's data validation scheme. When users enter invalid data in a worksheet, it is difficult to go back and check each cell manually.

Error Checking

If a cell contains a formula with an error, the top-left corner of the cell will contain a small triangle. Additionally, if you select a cell with an invalid formula, the Error Checking icon appears next to the cell. The Error Checking dialog box provides the name of the cell with the error, the type of error, details about the error, and various tools to help you fix the error.

How to Troubleshoot Invalid Data and Formulas
Procedure Reference: Troubleshoot Invalid Data

To troubleshoot invalid data:

1. On the Data tab, in the Data Tools group, from the Data Validation drop-down list, select Circle Invalid Data to circle the invalid data on the worksheet.
2. If necessary, in the Data Validation dialog box, on the Settings tab, select the type of data the cell can accept, and click OK.
3. Repair the data in the circled cell or cells so that it matches the data validation criteria.

Procedure Reference: Troubleshoot Invalid Formulas

To troubleshoot invalid formulas:

1. Open the Find And Replace dialog box.
2. On the Find tab, in the Find What text box, type # to search for cells with invalid formulas.
3. Expand Find Options by clicking the Options button.
4. From the Look In drop-down list, select Values.
5. Click Find All to list all of the cells that contain a pound sign (#) as hyperlinks at the bottom of the Find And Replace dialog box.
6. Click the hyperlink to the cell with the error you want to repair. Excel automatically advances to the cell.
7. In the worksheet, click the selected cell to activate the worksheet.

8. From the Error Checking drop-down list that appears next to the cell, select Edit In Formula Bar.

9. In the Formula bar, correct the formula.

10. In the Find And Replace dialog box, click the link to repair the next formula or click Close.

ACTIVITY 3-3

Troubleshooting Invalid Data and Formulas

Data Files:

Quarter Totals.xlsx

Before You Begin:

From C:\084892Data\Auditing Worksheets, open Quarter Totals.xlsx.

Scenario:

You have just completed developing a worksheet that tracks the total sales for the past two years made by the sales representatives in your company. Before sending the file for review, you decide to verify that all of the data and formulas in the file are valid. During this process you discover that the ID number for Leonard Simmonds is invalid. His actual ID number is 184533. You will also need to check for invalid formulas in the worksheet and fix them.

What You Do	How You Do It
1. **Locate the invalid data in the worksheet.**	a. On the Data tab, in the Data Tools group, **click the Data Validation button drop-down arrow and select Circle Invalid Data** to circle the invalid data in the worksheet.
	b. Observe that a red circle appears in cell A9 indicating invalid data.

	A	B	C	D	E	F	G
1	Average Rep/Year		$190,084.58				
2							
3	IDNumber	Last Name	First Initial	Year 1	Year 2	Total	Average Qt
4	105480	Arman	S	$214,815.00	$113,100.00	$327,915.00	$163,95
5	105608	Greenburg	L	$215,900.00	$122,700.00	$338,600.00	$169,30
6	110018	Lundquist	S	$125,000.00	$234,000.00	#NAME?	$179,50
7	147060	Unger	M	$123,300.00	$222,600.00	$345,900.00	$172.95
8	161975	Monder	A	$231,200.00	$223,100.00	$454,300.00	$227.15
9	Leonard	Simmonds	L	$230,900.00	$224,400.00	$455,300.00	$227.65
10							

	c. **Click cell A9.**
	d. In the Data Tools group, **click the Data Validation button drop-down arrow and select Data Validation.**
	e. In the Data Validation dialog box, on the Settings tab, **verify that the minimum value is set to 100000, and the maximum is set to 999999, and then click OK.**
	f. In cell A9, **type *184533* and press Enter.**

g. Observe that after entering valid data in the cell, the invalid data circle was removed automatically.

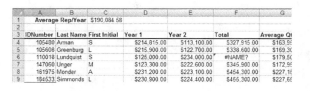

	A	B	C	D	E	F	G
1	Average Rep/Year		$190,084.58				
2							
3	IDNumber	Last Name	First Initial	Year 1	Year 2	Total	Average Qt
4	105480	Arman	S	$214,815.00	$113,100.00	$327,915.00	$163,95
5	105606	Greenburg	L	$215,900.00	$122,700.00	$338,600.00	$169,30
6	110018	Lundquist	S	$125,000.00	$234,000.00	#NAME?	$179,50
7	147060	Unger	M	$123,300.00	$222,600.00	$345,900.00	$172,95
8	161975	Monder	A	$231,200.00	$223,100.00	$454,300.00	$227,18
9	184533	Simmonds	L	$230,900.00	$224,400.00	$455,300.00	$227,65

2. Correct the invalid formulas.

a. On the Home tab, in the Editing group, **click Find & Select and choose Find.**

b. In the Find And Replace dialog box, in the Find What text box, **type #** to specify that you need to search for invalid formulas.

c. **Click Options** to expand the options in the Find And Replace dialog box.

d. From the Look In drop-down list, **select Values.**

e. **Click Find All.**

f. At the bottom of the Find And Replace dialog box, **verify that the first invalid formula is selected and that the cell in which the first instance of a pound sign in the worksheet has been selected.**

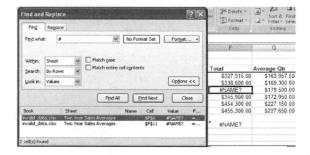

g. **Click the selected cell** to activate the worksheet.

h. In the worksheet, **move the mouse pointer over the Error Checking icon** and, from the Error Checking drop-down list next to the selected cell, **select Edit In Formula Bar.**

i. In the Formula bar, observe that the data range is not specified properly and **select E6F6** to change it to a valid formula.

j. **Type D6:E6 and press Enter** to correct the invalid formulas.

k. In the Find And Replace dialog box, **click Close.**

l. **Save the file as My Quarter Totals.xlsx and close it.**

TOPIC D
Watch and Evaluate Formulas

You have located invalid data and formulas in your workbook. Now, you have formulas that you need to continuously monitor. In this topic, you will watch and evaluate formulas.

Imagine a worksheet that contains complex formulas, many of which are off the viewable portion of your screen, when your focus is on a specific area of the worksheet. You need to view how certain formulas react to changes in the data, and verify that they are returning the results you expect even when you can't view the formulas on-screen because of the size of the worksheet. Watching and evaluating formulas enables you to monitor formulas during the development process, helping to ensure that formulas are functioning the way you want them to.

The Watch Window

The *Watch Window* allows you to view the contents of a cell while the cell itself is off the viewable portion of your screen. The Watch Window identifies the name of the workbook in which the cell appears, the name of the worksheet on which the cell lives, the cell reference, the value stored in the cell, and the formula, if any, that the cell contains.

Formula Evaluation

The Evaluate Formula dialog box displays the formula to be evaluated for the selected cell. The Evaluate button in the dialog box evaluates complex, nested formulas one action at a time, in the order of actions by which the formula is calculated. The most recent results appear italicized.

How to Watch and Evaluate Formulas
Procedure Reference: Watch Formulas

To watch formulas:
1. On the Formulas tab, in the Formula Auditing group, click Watch Window.
2. In the Watch Window, click Add Watch to display the Add Watch dialog box.
3. In the worksheet, select the cell or cells you want to watch.
4. In the Add Watch dialog box, click Add.
5. Make the necessary changes in the worksheet to update the data.
6. In the Watch Window, observe the corresponding change in data in the cells you want to watch.

Procedure Reference: Evaluate Formulas

To evaluate formulas:
1. On the worksheet, select the cell that contains the formula you want to evaluate.
2. On the Formulas tab, in the Formula Auditing group, click Evaluate Formula.
3. Click Evaluate to evaluate each portion of the formula in the order in which the formula is calculated. Repeat this step as often as needed to evaluate each step of the formula.
4. Close the Evaluate Formula dialog box.

ACTIVITY 3-4
Watching and Evaluating Formulas

Data Files:

Loan Schedule.xlsx

Before You Begin:

From C:\084892Data\Auditing Worksheets, open Loan Schedule.xlsx.

Scenario:

The Loan Schedule workbook tracks the amortization for loans that can be paid off in up to 60 months. You want to see the total interest that would be paid for payment terms of 24 and 36 months. Instead of scrolling down to the bottom of the worksheet every time you change the value in the Term In Months field to see the value, you decide to watch the cell that calculates the total interest paid. Additionally, you want to check whether the formula that calculates the principal amount works properly.

What You Do	How You Do It
1. **Add the cell with the total interest paid data to the Watch Window.**	a. On the Formulas tab, in the Formula Auditing group, **click Watch Window.**
	b. In the Watch Window, **click Add Watch.**
	c. In the worksheet, **scroll down and click cell D72.**
	d. In the Add Watch dialog box, **click Add** to add cell D72 to the Watch Window.
	e. Observe that the data in the Value column is 4,697.16.

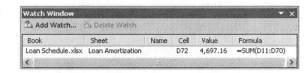

What You Do	How You Do It
2. **View the results in the Watch Window for loan repayment periods of 24 months.**	a. **Move the Watch Window to the bottom-left corner of the screen.**
	b. **Click cell D5.**
	c. **Type *24* and press Enter** to change the value of the cell.

d. In the Watch Window, observe that the data in the value column is displayed as 3,114.32 when the loan repayment period is mentioned as 24 months.

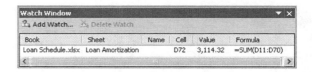

e. In cell D5, **type** *36* **and press Enter.**

f. In the Watch Window, observe that the data in the Value column is reverted to 4,697.16.

g. **Close the Watch Window.**

3. **Evaluate the formula for the first instance of the remaining principal amount.**

a. **Click cell F11.**

b. In the Formula Auditing group, **click Evaluate Formula.**

c. In the Evaluate Formula dialog box, in the Evaluation text box, observe that cells B11, D5, C11, and E11 are included in the formula.

d. In the worksheet, observe that the value of cell B11 is 1, which will be substituted in the evaluation formula. In the Evaluate Formula dialog box, **click Evaluate.**

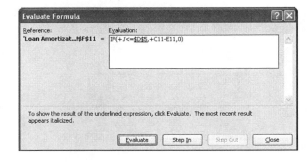

e. **Click Evaluate** to substitute the value in cell D5.

f. **Click Evaluate** to evaluate the expression, 1<=36.

g. Observe that the condition less-than-or-equal-to is TRUE, and **click Evaluate** to substitute the value in cell C11.

h. **Click Evaluate** to substitute the value in cell E11.

i. **Click Evaluate** to show the result of the underlined expression.

j. **Click Evaluate** to evaluate the final expression that is underlined.

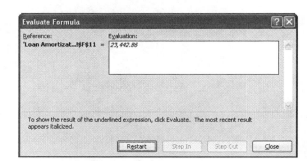

k. Observe that the first value in the IF function is TRUE, and therefore, the function would return the second value as the result and **click Close.**

l. **Save the file as *My Loan Schedule Watch.xlsx* and close it.**

TOPIC E
Create a Data List Outline

You have watched and evaluated formulas in order to closely monitor the data that was not within the view area. You have both individual data and data lists in your worksheet, and now you want to view only the data lists by themselves. In this topic, you will create a data list outline.

Viewing the data lists in a clear format can be a very effective means of analyzing and comparing a subset of data to the entire worksheet or workbook. But what if you want to view several data lists side by side and compare them? Data list outlines allow you to view multiple data lists at the same time.

Outlines

Definition:

An *outline* is a data organizing method in which a set of data is combined to form a group. Data in a worksheet must be sorted before it can be outlined. Once the groups are created, they can be expanded or collapsed as necessary. An outline can have one group or multiple groups.

Example:

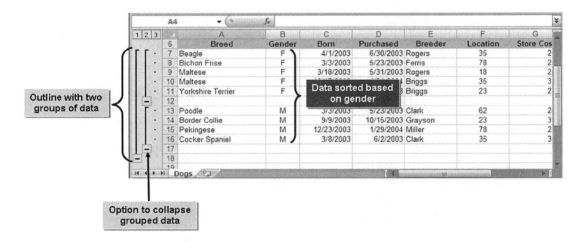

The Outline Group

The Outline group located on the data tab contains options to group, ungroup, and subtotal the data in the worksheet.

Option	Description
Group	Combines a range of cells so that it is possible to collapse or expand them. The Group drop-down list has two options: Group and Auto Outline. The Group option groups the data by either row or column, and the Auto Outline option groups the data automatically based on the type of data.
Ungroup	Ungroups the grouped range of cells.
Subtotal	Totals data between rows by inserting subtotals and grand totals for the selected cells automatically.

How to Create a Data List Outline

Procedure Reference: Group and Outline Data Using Auto Outline

To group and outline data using Auto Outline:

1. In the desired file, sort the list by criterion of your choice.
2. Select the range of cells that has to be outlined.
3. On the Data tab, in the Outline group, from the Group drop-down list, select Auto Outline to automatically group and outline the data.
4. If necessary, collapse the details.

Procedure Reference: Group and Outline Data Using the Group Option

To group and outline data using the Group option:

1. In the desired file, sort the list by criterion of your choice.
2. Select the rows or columns you want to group.
3. On the Data tab, in the Outline group, from the Group drop-down list, select Group to manually group and outline the data.
4. If necessary, collapse the details.

Procedure Reference: Add Subtotals to Grouped Data Using the Subtotal Option

To add subtotals to grouped data using the Subtotal option:

1. Open the file with the data that has been grouped.
2. Select the range of cells that has to be subtotaled.

3.   On the Data tab, in the Outline group, click Subtotal to calculate the subtotal and add it to the grouped data.

ACTIVITY 3-5

Creating a Data List Outline

Data Files:

Dogs.xlsx

Before You Begin:

From C:\084892Data\Auditing Worksheets, open Dogs.xlsx.

Scenario:

The northeast regional manager would like to compare the average store cost of female and male dogs to the total average. He asked if you can put the information in the Dogs workbook in an outline for him so that he can easily see the averages.

What You Do	How You Do It
1. Sort the data by gender.	a. **Click cell B6.**
	b. On the Home tab, in the Editing group, **click Sort & Filter and choose Sort A To Z.**
	c. **Right-click row 16 heading and choose Insert** to separate the female dogs data from the male dogs data with a new row.
2. Create three averages: one for the store cost of female dogs, another for the store cost of male dogs, and the last for the overall store cost of both.	a. In cell A23, **type *Average Female Dog Cost* and press Enter.**
	b. **Click cell G23.**
	c. In the Formula bar, **type =AVERAGE(G7:G15) and press Enter** to calculate the average female dog cost.
	d. **Calculate the average male dog cost by typing *Average Male Dog Cost* in cell A24, and calculate the average of the range G17:G21 in cell G24.**
	e. **Calculate the overall average dog cost by typing *Overall Average Dog Cost* in cell A25, and calculate the average of the range G7:G21 in cell G25.**

3. **Create individual groups for the female dogs, the male dogs, and the averages.**

    a. **Click cell A7.**

    b. On the Data tab, in the Outline group, **click the Group button drop-down arrow and select Auto Outline** to automatically group the cells.

    c. At the left side of the worksheet, observe that separate outlines are created for the average female, average male, and overall average dog costs.

    d. **Select rows 7 to 15** to select the female dogs.

    e. In the Outline group, **click the Group button drop-down arrow and select Group.**

4. **Collapse the details so that only the averages for female dog, male dog, and overall dog costs are shown.**

    a. To the left of row heading 16, **click the minus sign** to collapse the female dog list.

    b. To the left of row heading 23, **click the minus sign** to collapse the male dog list.

    c. Observe that the average cost of female and male dogs, along with the overall dog cost is displayed in the worksheet.

    d. **Save the file as *My Dogs.xlsx* and close the workbook.**

ACTIVITY 3-6
Adding Subtotals to Grouped Data

Data Files:

Grouped Dogs.xlsx

Before You Begin:

From C:\084892Data\Auditing Worksheets, open Grouped Dogs.xlsx.

Scenario:

You have calculated the total cost of all the dogs in the store. The regional manager would like to get the total cost of each female breed of dog alone.

What You Do	How You Do It
1. **Display the Subtotal dialog box.**	a. **Select the range A6:H18.**
	b. On the Data tab, in the Outline group, **click Subtotal.**
2. **Subtotal the store cost of female breed dogs.**	a. In the Subtotal dialog box, in the At Each Change In drop-down list box, **verify that Breed is selected.**
	b. In the Add Subtotal To list box, **uncheck the Price check box.**
	c. **Check the Store Cost check box and click OK.**
	d. **Resize Column A** so that the breed names are completely displayed.
	e. **Verify that the subtotals are calculated for the store cost of female breed dogs.**
	f. **Save the file as *My Grouped Dogs.xlsx* and close it.**

Lesson 3 Follow-up

In this lesson, you audited worksheets. By auditing worksheets you can verify data validity and ensure that formulas, functions, and data all work together in the way you intended.

1. **What auditing features will you use in your workbooks?**

2. **How might you incorporate auditing features into an overall workbook development process that helps minimize errors?**

4 | Analyzing Data

Lesson Time: 45 minutes

Lesson Objectives:

In this lesson, you will analyze data.

You will:

- Create a trendline.
- Create scenarios.
- Perform what-if analysis.
- Perform statistical analysis with the Analysis ToolPak.

Introduction

You audited worksheets and ensured that formulas, functions, and data all work together in the way you intended. Now you need to make use of the data to make business decisions. In this lesson, you will analyze data.

You can work efficiently with Microsoft® Office Excel® by using the application for analyzing data. Analyzing data brings more value out of the data than if the data was simply stored.

TOPIC A

Create a Trendline

You have a worksheet that contains a chart. You now want to forecast future values based on the chart data. In this topic, you will create a trendline.

You want to predict the potential sales growth of your company for the next four quarters. Instead of using a worksheet that does not make projections, you may want to use a worksheet that projects sales for the next four quarters. Trendlines graphically forecast data to help make predictive business decisions.

Trendlines

Definition:

A *trendline* is a graphical representation of trends in a data series that allows you to study predictions in data. They are usually represented by a line. These trendlines are particularly useful in depicting trends in existing data or forecasting future data. Trendlines can be added to data series in column, line, bar, area, stock, or bubble charts. Trendlines can be created using default settings or by specifying user-defined settings.

Example:

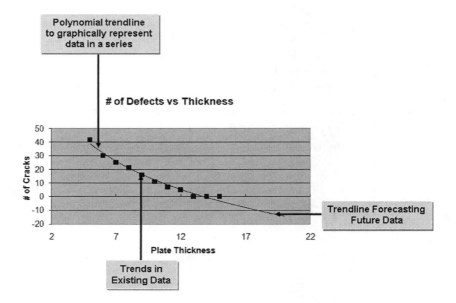

Trendline Types

There are six different types of trendlines that can be used to study predictions in data.

Trendline Type	Description
Exponential	Curved lines that are best used when data values rise or fall at increasingly higher rates.
Linear	Straight lines that are best used with linear data sets.
Logarithmic	Curved lines that are best used when the rate of change in the data increases or decreases quickly and finally levels out.
Polynomial	Curved lines that are best used when the data fluctuates with ups and downs.
Power	Curved lines that are best used with data sets, which compare measurements that increase at a specified rate.
Moving Average	Curved lines that are used to smooth out any fluctuations in data, thereby displaying a pattern in the data.

How to Create a Trendline

Procedure Reference: Create a Trendline with Default Settings

To create a trendline with default settings:

1. In the chart that contains the data to which you want to apply a trendline, select the series of data you want to plot on a trendline.
2. On the Chart Tools Layout contextual tab, in the Analysis group, from the Trendline drop-down list, select a trendline type.

Procedure Reference: Create a Trendline with User-Defined Settings

To create a trendline with user-defined settings:

1. In the chart that contains the data to which you want to apply a trendline, select the series of data you want to plot on a trendline.
2. Display the Format Trendline dialog box.
   - On the Chart Tools Layout contextual tab, in the Analysis group, from the Trendline drop-down list, select More Trendline Options.
   - Or, right-click the data series and choose Add Trendline.
3. In the Format Trendline dialog box, in the Trend/Regression Type section, select the type of trendline you want.
4. If necessary, in the Trendline Name section, specify a name for the trendline.
   - Select the Automatic option in order to give the trendline an automatic name.
   - Or, select the Custom option, and in the Custom text box, type a name for the trendline.

5. In the Forecast section, specify the desired settings.

- In the Forward text box, type the desired value to determine how far ahead you want to forecast.

- In the Backward text box, type the desired value to determine how far behind you want to forecast.

6. If necessary, in the left pane, select Line Color and specify the line color for the trendline.

7. If necessary, select Line Style and specify the line style for the trendline.

8. If necessary, select Shadow and apply the desired shadow effect for the trendline.

9. Click Close.

ACTIVITY 4-1

Creating a Trendline

Data Files:

Pottery Performance.xlsx

Before You Begin:

From C:\084892Data\Analyzing Data, open Pottery Performance.xlsx.

Scenario:

You need to forecast the thickness of plates which, when manufactured, will be of good quality and will have fewer cracks. You have a scatter plot chart to use for your reports. You find that there is a sudden decrease in the value in the chart, and then it levels out. You need to forecast the data graphically by applying a dark red color and a dash style.

What You Do	How You Do It
1. Add a trendline that will forecast the plate thickness data forward five units.	a. In the workbook, **select the Scatter Plot worksheet tab.**
	b. In the scatter plot chart, **click the first value at the intersection of (5,42)** to select the data series.

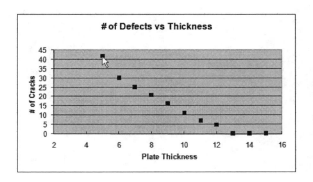

c. **Select the Chart Tools Layout contextual tab.**

d. In the Analysis group, **click Trendline and choose More Trendline Options.**

e. In the Format Trendline dialog box, in the Trend/Regression Type section, **select the Logarithmic option.**

f. In the Forecast section, in the Forward text box, **triple-click and type 5**

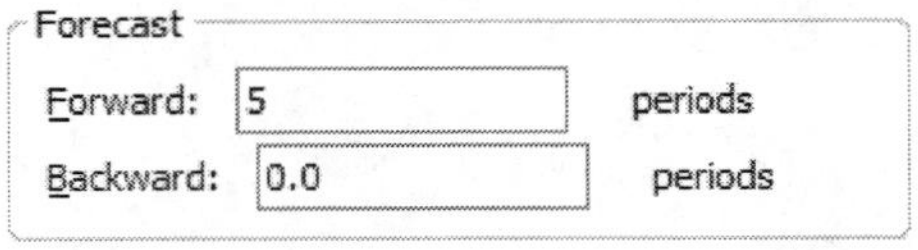

Forecast
| | |
Forward: 5   periods
Backward: 0.0   periods

g. **Click Close** to close the Format Trendline dialog box.

---

2. **True or False? The trendline suggests that plate thicknesses of 13 or greater will result in 0 (zero) or fewer cracks.**

___ True

___ False

---

3. **Apply line color and line style to the trendline.**

a. **Display the Format Trendline dialog box.**

b. In the left pane, **select Line Color.**

c. In the right pane, **select the Solid Line option.**

d. **Click Color** and in the Standard Colors section, **select the first option** to apply Dark Red.

e. In the left pane, **select Line Style.**

f. In the right pane, **click Dash Type and select the last option** to apply the Long Dash Dot Dot style and **click Close.**

g. Notice that the chart displays a trendline with the specified settings.

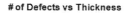

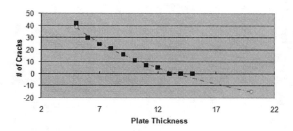

h. **Save the file as *My Pottery Performance.xlsx* and close it.**

TOPIC B

Create Scenarios

You created trendlines to forecast future values based on the chart data. You would now like to alter data to help forecast different values based on criteria you set. In this topic, you will create scenarios.

You have a worksheet that calculates mortgage payments. You would like to see what would happen to your monthly payments if you decreased the interest rate by one or more points and increased the number of months to pay off by 12. At the same time, you do not want to delete the original values in the worksheet. Scenarios help you forecast a particular outcome and plan accordingly.

Scenarios

Definition:

A *scenario* is a set of input values that are substituted for the primary data in a worksheet. These input values are used to forecast new values based on the data that represents the sample situation in your worksheet. You can create any number of scenarios in a worksheet and can switch between them to view the results of the corresponding scenario.

Example:

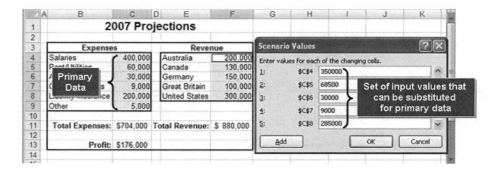

The What-If Analysis Option

The What-If Analysis option is used to perform analysis using the Scenario Manager, Goal Seek, and Data Table.

Option	Description
Scenario Manager	An option that is used to create scenarios.
Goal Seek	An option that is used to set the value stored in a single cell to a specific value, thereby changing the value stored in another cell.
Data Table	An option that is used to display the varying results of formulas based on different values given as input.

The Scenario Manager Dialog Box

The Scenario Manager dialog box allows you to create, edit, delete, and merge scenarios.

Option	*Description*
Scenarios	Lists all the scenarios you have created in the worksheet.
Add	Invokes the Add Scenario dialog box that allows you to create a new scenario.
Delete	Deletes the selected scenario.
Edit	Invokes the Edit Scenario dialog box that allows you to edit a scenario.
Merge	Allows you to merge scenarios from other worksheets.
Summary	Displays a summary of the scenario in the Scenario Summary dialog box.
Changing Cells	Displays the cell reference for changing cells.
Comment	Displays the comments entered in the Add Scenario dialog box.
Show	Displays the result of the selected scenario on the worksheet.

How to Create Scenarios

Procedure Reference: Create a Scenario

To create a scenario:

1. Select a range for which you want to create a scenario.
2. On the Data tab, in the Data Tools group, from the What-If Analysis drop-down list, select Scenario Manager.
3. In the Scenario Manager dialog box, click Add.
4. In the Add Scenario dialog box, in the Scenario Name text box, type a name for the scenario.
5. If necessary, add a comment in the Comment text box, and then click OK.
6. In the Scenario Values dialog box, change the values as appropriate.
7. Click OK to create the scenario.
8. In the Scenario Manager dialog box, click Close.

ACTIVITY 4-2
Creating Scenarios

Data Files:

2007 Projections.xlsx

Before You Begin:

From C:\084892Data\Analyzing Data open 2007 Projections.xlsx.

Scenario:

You would like to analyze the expense and revenue data of the previous year, and want to forecast a particular outcome and plan accordingly for the current year. You would like to retain the value of the existing data and compare this with a situation where the advertising budget is increased by $40,000 and each country's revenue by 10 percent.

What You Do	How You Do It
1. Create a scenario that maintains the original projection numbers for 2007.	a. **Select the range C4:C9.**
	b. **Hold down Ctrl and click cell F4.**
	c. **Hold down Shift and click cell F8** to select the range F4:F8.
	d. On the Data tab, in the Data Tools group, **click What-If Analysis and choose Scenario Manager.**
	e. In the Scenario Manager dialog box, **click Add.**
	f. In the Add Scenario dialog box, in the Scenario Name text box, **type *2007 Original Projections***
	g. **Select the content in the Comment text box.**

h. **Replace the text with** *This scenario illustrates the original 2007 projections*

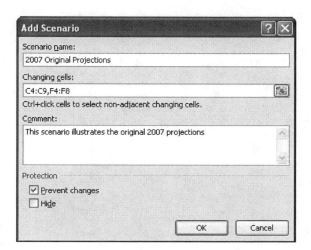

i. **Click OK.**

j. In the Scenario Values dialog box, **click OK** to accept the current values and to return to the Scenario Manager dialog box.

2. **Create another scenario to specify the values for the first range of cells.**

   a. In the Scenario Manager dialog box, **click Add.**

   b. In the Add Scenario dialog box, in the Scenario Name text box, **type** *2007 Advertising Push*

   c. **Select the content in the Comment text box.**

   d. **Replace the text with** *This scenario increases the advertising budget to 40,000 and each country's revenue by 10%*

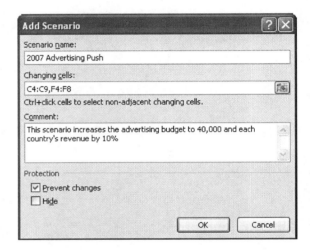

   e. **Click OK.**

   f. In the Scenario Values dialog box displaying the values for the first range of cells, in the third text box, **double-click and type** *40000*

3. **Specify the values for the second range of cells.**

   a. In the dialog box, **scroll down** to view the values in the second range of cells, F4:F8.

   b. **Select the value in the $F$4 text box and type** *220000*

c. **Change the remaining values in the Scenario Values dialog box as follows:**

$F$5: 143000

$F$6: 165000

$F$7: 110000

$F$8: 330000

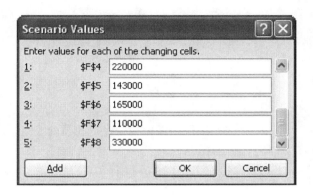

d. **Click OK.**

e. In the Scenario Manager dialog box, **click Close.**

---

4. Test your work.

a. On the Data tab, in the Data Tools section, **click What-If Analysis and choose Scenario Manager.**

b. **Verify that 2007 Advertising Push is selected and click Show.**

c. Notice that the values in the workbook change and the workbook displays the new scenario.

Expenses		Revenue	
Salaries	400,000	Australia	220,000
Rent/Utilities	60,000	Canada	143,000
Advertising	40,000	Germany	165,000
Office Expenses	9,000	Great Britain	110,000
Liability Insurance	200,000	United States	330,000
Other	5,000		
Total Expenses:	$ 714,000	Total Revenue:	$ 968,000
Profit:	$ 254,000		

d. In the Scenario Manager dialog box, in the Scenarios list box, **select 2007 Original Projections and click Show.**

e. Notice that the values in the workbook revert to the original values.

Expenses		Revenue	
Salaries	400,000	Australia	200,000
Rent/Utilities	60,000	Canada	130,000
Advertising	30,000	Germany	150,000
Office Expenses	9,000	Great Britain	100,000
Liability Insurance	200,000	United States	300,000
Other	5,000		
Total Expenses: $	704,000	Total Revenue: $	880,000
Profit: $	176,000		

f. In the Scenario Manager dialog box, **click Close.**

g. **Save the file as** *My 2007 Projections.xlsx* **and close it.**

TOPIC C
Perform What-If Analysis

You analyzed data using trendlines and scenarios. You now want to forecast potential values by changing variables in formulas without affecting your original data. In this topic, you will perform what-if analysis.

You have a worksheet that can calculate the monthly payments on a mortgage. You want to change the monthly payment value from $700 per month to $800 per month to see how the increased payment might affect the overall length of the loan term. By using what-if analysis, you can make this type of projection without having to rewrite a formula.

The Solver Option

The *Solver* option is used to set the value stored in a single cell that has a formula, to a specified value by changing the value stored in multiple other cells. This option allows you to either retain the Solver solution or restore the original values.

Example of Solver

Consider that you have planned to borrow money to get an all-terrain vehicle for yourself. You are sure that you can afford a monthly payment of $400 as long as the interest rate is 12 percent. Using Solver, you can calculate the amount you can borrow for the specified constraints.

The Solver Parameters Dialog Box

The Solver Parameters dialog box has a number of options that can be used to set the solver parameters.

Option	Description
Set Target Cell	Used to enter the cell reference or name for the target cell. The target cell is a cell that will contain the result of the evaluation.
Equal To	Used to display the maximum, minimum, or a certain value in the target cell.
By Changing Cells	Used to enter a cell reference or a name that needs to be adjusted. Adjustable cells are cells that contain values that will change based on specified criteria.
Guess	Used to specify the adjustable cells. The Solver guesses the adjustable cells based on the target cell.
Subject To The Constraints	Used to view the constraints that have been created. Constrained cells are cells that meet a specified criterion prior to the evaluation taking place, and they can be a number, a cell reference, or a formula.
Add	Used to display the Add Constraints dialog box, which helps you create a constraint.
Options	Used to display the Solver Options dialog box, which helps you load and save problem models. Advanced features of the solution process can also be controlled by using this dialog box.

How to Perform What-If Analysis

Procedure Reference: Perform What-If Analysis Using Goal Seek

To perform what-if analysis using Goal Seek:

1. On the Data tab, in the Data Tools group, from the What-If Analysis drop-down list, select Goal Seek.

2. In the Goal Seek dialog box, in the Set Cell text box, enter the cell reference whose value should remain unchanged.

3. In the To Value text box, type the value for the set cell.

4. In the By Changing Cell text box, enter the cell reference for which you need to change the value and click OK.

5. In the Goal Seek Status dialog box, click OK to accept the solution.

Procedure Reference: Load the Solver Add-In

To load the Solver Add-In:

1. Display the Excel Options dialog box.

2. In the left pane, select Add-Ins.

3. If necessary, in the right pane, from the Manage drop-down list, select Excel Add-Ins and then click Go.

4. In the Add-Ins dialog box, in the Add-Ins Available list box, check the Solver Add-In check box and click OK.

5. Click Yes to install the Solver Add-In.

Procedure Reference: Perform What-If Analysis Using Solver

To perform what-if analysis using Solver:

1. Open an existing worksheet.

2. On the Data tab, in the Analysis group, click Solver.

3. In the Solver Parameters dialog box, in the Set Target Cell text box, enter the cell reference of the target cell for which the value should remain unchanged.

4. In the Equal To section, select an option and specify the value for the target cell.

5. In the By Changing Cells text box, enter the cell references that Solver can change to produce the desired outcome.

6. In the Subject To The Constraints section, click Add.

7. In the Add Constraint dialog box, add the constraints that need to be applied to the changing cells.

8. Add the constraint to the Subject To The Constraints section.

    *   Click Add to add the current constraint and to proceed with the steps to add another.

    *   Or, click OK to add the constraint and to return to the Solver Parameters dialog box.

9. In the Solver Parameters dialog box, click Solve.

10. In the Solver Results dialog box, click OK.

ACTIVITY 4-3

Using Goal Seek to Analyze Data

Data Files:

Loan Schedule.xlsx

Before You Begin:

From C:\084892Data\Analyzing Data, open Loan Schedule.xlsx.

Scenario:

You have developed a worksheet named Loan Schedule that amortizes a car loan. The worksheet currently amortizes a $24,000 loan over 60 months with a 12 percent interest rate. However, after reviewing some of your other monthly expenses, you have come to realize that you can only afford a $17,500 loan with a monthly payment set at $350.00. You need to determine the term of the loan based on this new data.

What You Do	How You Do It
1. Decrease the value of the principal loan amount.	a. Click cell D3 and press Delete.
	b. Type *17500* and press Enter.

2. **Find the new loan term for the defined principal amount and monthly payment of $350.**

a. On the Data tab, in the Data Tools group, from the What-If Analysis drop-down list, **choose Goal Seek.**

b. In the Goal Seek dialog box, in the Set Cell text box, **type *F4* and press Tab.**

c. In the To Value text box, **type *350* to set** the monthly payment amount.

d. In the By Changing Cell text box, **type *D5* and click OK.**

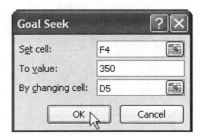

e. In the Goal Seek Status dialog box, **click OK.**

f. Notice that the new loan term displayed in cell D5 is 69.66 months.

g. **Save the file as *My Loan Schedule.xlsx***

ACTIVITY 4-4

Using Solver to Analyze Data

Before You Begin:

My Loan Schedule.xlsx is open.

Scenario:

A windfall has come your way and you can now afford to spend a little more on your new car. Based on other expenses in your long-term budget, you have decided that you can now afford a $500 monthly payment as long as the interest rate stays between 10 and 15 percent, and your payments are for less than 36 months. Now, you want to find out how much you can borrow.

What You Do	How You Do It
1. Load the Solver Add-In.	a. **Display the Excel Options dialog box.**
	b. In the left pane, **select the Add-Ins category.**
	c. At the bottom of the right pane, **verify that Excel Add-Ins is selected from the Manage drop-down list.**
	d. To the right of the Manage drop-down list, **click Go.**
	e. In the Add-Ins dialog box, **check the Solver Add-In check box and click OK.**
	f. **Click Yes** to install the Solver Add-In.
2. Change the monthly payment from $350 to $500.	a. In the worksheet, **click cell F4.**
	b. On the Data tab, in the Analysis group, **click Solver.**

c. In the Solver Parameters dialog box, in the Set Target Cell text box, observe that the target cell is $F$4.

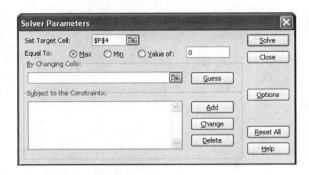

d. **Select the Value Of option.**

e. In the Value Of text box, **double-click and type 500**

---

3. **Specify the cells with the principal amount value, interest rate, and term in months as changing cells.**

   a. **Click in the By Changing Cells text box.**

   b. **Type D3, D4, D5**

---

4. **Add constraints to set the interest rate between 10 to 15 percent, and the term to be less than 35 months.**

   a. In the Subject To The Constraints section, **click Add.**

   b. In the Add Constraint dialog box, in the Cell Reference text box, **type D4**

   c. From the drop-down list to the right of the Cell Reference text box, **select >=.**

d. In the Constraint text box, **type *10%* and click Add.**

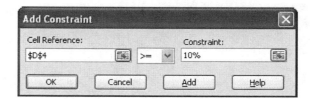

e. In the Cell Reference text box, **type *D4***

f. **Verify that <= is selected in the drop-down list box** and, in the Constraint text box, **type *15%* and click Add.**

g. In the Cell Reference text box, **type *D5***

h. **Verify that <= is selected in the drop-down list box** and, in the Constraint text box, **type *35***

i. In the Add Constraint dialog box, **click OK.**

j. In the Subject To The Constraints list box, notice that the specified constraints are listed.

5. **Calculate the new principal amount.**

a. In the Solver Parameters dialog box, **click Solve to run the Solver.**

b. In the Solver Results dialog box, **click OK** to keep the Solver solution.

c. Notice that the principal amount is changed to 15124.75.

Principal Amount:	15124.75	Monthly Payment
Interest Rate:	10%	$500.00
Term in Months:	35.00	

d. **Save and close the file.**

TOPIC D

Perform Statistical Analysis with the Analysis ToolPak

You performed what-if analysis to make projections based on existing data. Now you need to analyze complex data to provide new insights into data that could not have been derived from Excel's standard functions. In this topic, you will perform statistical analysis with the Analysis ToolPak.

You have a workbook with a complex data set. Performing statistical analysis using the tools available in the Analysis ToolPak helps you derive the desired value from complex data sets.

The Analysis ToolPak

The Analysis ToolPak is an add-in that contains a wide variety of tools to help you perform sophisticated statistical analysis. This includes tools to create histograms, derive random samples, and perform regression analysis.

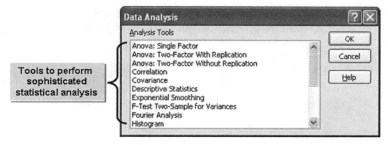

Figure 4-1: The tools in the Analysis ToolPak.

How to Perform Statistical Analysis with the Analysis ToolPak

Procedure Reference: Load the Analysis ToolPak

To load the Analysis ToolPak:

1. In the Excel Options dialog box, in the left pane, select Add-Ins.
2. If necessary, in the right pane, from the Manage drop-down list, select Excel Add-ins and then click Go.
3. In the Add-Ins dialog box, check the Analysis ToolPak check box and click OK.

Procedure Reference: Perform Statistical Analysis with the Analysis ToolPak

To perform statistical analysis with the Analysis ToolPak:

1. On the Data tab, in the Analysis group, click Data Analysis.
2. In the Data Analysis dialog box, select the desired data analysis tool and click OK.
3. In the dialog box that opens for the tool you selected, set the values and options you want and click OK.

Procedure Reference: Use the Sampling Analysis Tool for Performing Analysis

To use the Sampling analysis tool for performing analysis:

1. On the Data tab, in the Analysis group, click Data Analysis.

2. In the Data Analysis dialog box, in the Analysis Tools list box, select Sampling and click OK.

3. In the Sampling dialog box, in the Input section, in the Input Range text box, enter the cell reference for the range of data for which you want to perform the analysis.

4. If necessary, check the Labels check box if you want to include the first row or column of input range as labels in the sample.

5. In the Sampling Method section, select the desired option.

   - Select the Periodic option and enter the value in the Period text box, to indicate a periodic interval at which you want sampling to happen.

   - Or, select the Random option and enter the value in the Number Of Samples text box that you want to display in the output column.

6. In the Output Options section, select the desired option.

   - Select the Output Range option, and in the Output Range text box, enter the cell reference for the output.

   - Select the New Worksheet Ply option in order to insert and display the results in a new worksheet in the workbook beginning at cell A1. If necessary, in the New Worksheet Ply text box, type the desired name for the sheet.

   - Or, select the New Workbook option in order to display the results in a new workbook.

7. Click OK.

ACTIVITY 4-5

Performing Statistical Analysis with the Analysis ToolPak

Data Files:

Randomize.xlsx

Before You Begin:

From C:\084892Data\Analyzing Data, open Randomize.xlsx.

Scenario:

Your company has collected the names of 60 people who are willing to participate in a focus group to help you refine your flagship product. However, you can only have 10 people in the focus group. The team overseeing the focus group needs a way to randomly select 10 people from the list of 60. The random list needs to include the focus group candidates' ID number and last name.

What You Do	How You Do It
1. Load the Analysis ToolPak add-in.	a. In the Excel Options dialog box, in the left pane, **select the Add-Ins category.**
	b. **Verify that Excel Add-ins is selected in the Manage drop-down list box.**
	c. In the right pane, to the right of the Manage drop-down list, **click Go.**
	d. In the Add-Ins dialog box, in the Add-Ins Available section, **check the Analysis ToolPak check box and click OK.**
	e. **Click Yes** to install the Analysis ToolPak add-in.
2. Open the Sampling analysis tool.	a. On the Data tab, in the Analysis group, **click Data Analysis.**
	b. In the Data Analysis dialog box, in the Analysis Tools list box, **scroll down and select Sampling and click OK.**

3. In a new worksheet, **create a random sample of 10 people.**

a. In the Sampling dialog box, in the Input section, in the Input Range text box, **type *A2:A61*** to specify the range of people.

b. In the Sampling Method section, in the Number Of Samples text box, **type *10***

c. In the Output Options section, in the New Worksheet Ply text box, **type *Focus Group Sample***

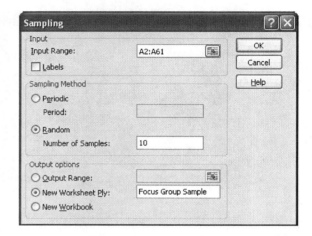

d. **Click OK.**

4. In the new worksheet, **look up the last name of each unique ID.**

   a. **Click cell B1.**

   b. On the Formulas tab, in the Function Library group, **click Lookup & Reference and choose VLOOKUP.**

   c. In the Function Arguments dialog box, in the Lookup_value text box, **type *A1*** to find the last name of the first column in the table.

   d. In the Table_array text box, **type *'Focus Group Candidates'!$A$2:$C$61*** to include the data from the specified range in the Focus Group Candidates worksheet.

   e. In the Col_index_num text box, **type *3*** to display the data in column 3 corresponding to the Focus Group Candidates worksheet.

   f. In the Range_lookup text box, **type *False*** to find the exact match and **click OK.**

   g. Notice that the last name of the first unique ID is displayed.

5. **Display the last name for all the unique IDs in the worksheet.**

   a. **Drag the fill handle from cell B1 to cell B10** to display the last name of the candidates.

   b. **Save the workbook as *My Randomize* and then close the file.**

Lesson 4 Follow-up

In this lesson, you analyzed data. Analyzing data brings more value out of the data than if the data was simply stored and never looked at again.

1. **What projects are you currently working on that would benefit from the creation of trendlines?**

2. **How might you deploy Scenarios, Goal Seek, and Solver into your current projects?**

5 | Working with Multiple Workbooks

Lesson Time: 35 minutes

Lesson Objectives:

In this lesson, you will work with multiple workbooks.

You will:

- Create a workspace.
- Consolidate data.
- Link cells in different workbooks.
- Edit links.

Introduction

You stored and analyzed data in a single workbook. Now you would like to refer to and work with data in more than one workbook. In this lesson, you will work with multiple workbooks.

Having created multiple workbooks, you find it difficult to open each workbook separately when you need to refer to particular data. The workbooks share the same data and you feel that it would be better if you could consolidate and link data in one workbook with another. You can use a single Microsoft® Office Excel® file as a repository for data from multiple workbooks.

TOPIC A

Create a Workspace

You analyzed data in a workbook. It would be convenient if you could open a set of workbooks with the size and position intact whenever you require them in your calculations. In this topic, you will create a workspace to manage data across multiple workbooks.

You have 10 workbooks that share related data. You are constantly working on all 10, and you have long felt that it would be easier to manage all of the data if you could consolidate all of the workbooks into a single source file. You decide to create a workspace that includes all of the related workbooks. By creating a workspace, you can easily manage related sets of data that span across multiple workbooks.

Workspaces

Definition:

A *workspace* is an Excel file that contains location, screen size, and screen position data about multiple workbooks. Workspace files are saved with the .xlw extension. A single workspace file can open multiple workbook files at a time.

Example:

employee_data
.xlw

Workspace files are saved
with .xlw extension

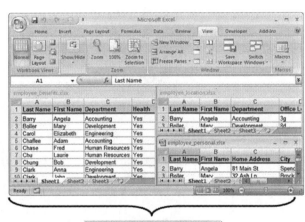

A workspace containing the
location, screen size, and
screen position data of
multiple workbooks

How to Create a Workspace

Procedure Reference: Create a Workspace

To create a workspace:

1. Open all the files that you want to include in a workbook.
2. Size and position the workbooks as you would like them to appear.
3. Arrange the windows.
4. On the View tab, in the Window group, click Save Workspace.
5. In the Save Workspace dialog box, in the File Name text box, type the desired name.
6. Click Save to save the file with the .xlw extension.

ACTIVITY 5-1

Creating a Workspace

Data Files:

Employee Personal.xlsx, Employee Benefits.xlsx, Employee Location.xlsx

Before You Begin:

From C:\084892Data\Working with Multiple Workbooks, open Employee Personal.xlsx, Employee Benefits.xlsx, and Employee Location.xlsx.

Scenario:

You are in charge of updating employee information that is stored in three different workbooks. You have found that as your company grows, you are using these three workbooks together all the time. You want to create a single source that can open all three workbooks at the same time, with the display intact, whenever required.

What You Do	How You Do It
1. **Arrange all open windows vertically.**	a. On the View tab, in the Window group, **click Arrange All.**
	b. In the Arrange Windows dialog box, in the Arrange section, **select Vertical.**
	c. **Click OK.**
2. **Create a workspace.**	a. In the Window group, **click Save Workspace.**
	b. **Navigate to C:\084892Data\Working with Multiple Workbooks.**
	c. In the Save Workspace dialog box, in the File Name text box, **type Workspace Employee Data**
	d. Notice that the file type displayed in the Save As Type drop-down list box is Workspaces (*.xlw) **and click Save.**

3. **Test your work.**

    a. **Close all the open workbooks.**

    b. **Click the Office button and choose Open.**

    c. In the Open dialog box, **select Workspace Employee Data.xlw and click Open.**

    d. Notice that the files are arranged in the same sequence, position, and size.

    e. **Close all the open windows.**

TOPIC B
Consolidate Data

You have created a workspace which includes multiple workbooks sharing the related data. You want to summarize the data from multiple workbooks into a single worksheet. In this topic, you will consolidate the data.

You have 10 workbooks which share related data. Your manager wants to see a summary of all that data, but she doesn't want to open all 10 workbooks and read individual summaries. You consolidate the data from the 10 workbooks into a single worksheet that your manager can easily access. Consolidating data from multiple workbooks into a single worksheet helps the analysis process by summarizing large amounts of data in a single interface.

Data Consolidation

Definition:

Data consolidation is the method of summarizing data from several ranges into a single range. The data range can be from the same worksheet, the same workbook, or from different workbooks. You can consolidate data by position, when the data has an identical structure, or you can also consolidate data by category, when the data is similar but in different relative locations.

Example:

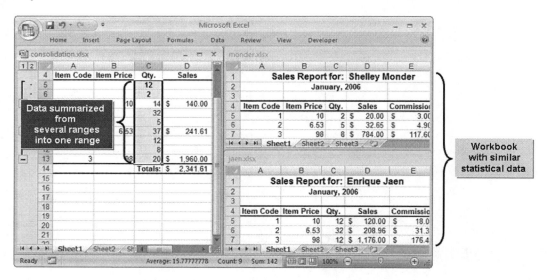

The Consolidate Dialog Box

The Consolidate dialog box can be displayed by clicking Consolidate in the Data Tools group of the Data tab. This dialog box has a number of options that can be used to consolidate data.

Option	*Description*
Function	A drop-down list that lists all the available built-in functions.
Reference	A text box that can be used to enter the cell reference for the cell or for the range.
Browse	A button that can be used to browse, if data is present in another workbook.
All References	A list box where all the existing references are listed.
Add	A button that can be used to add a reference which has been entered in the References text box, to the All References list box.
Delete	A button that can be used to delete a cell reference that has been added to the All References list box.
Use Labels In	A section that is used to specify the location of the labels in the source range—either in the top row or in the left column.
Create Links To Source Data	A check box that can be used to create links to source data.

How to Consolidate Data

Procedure Reference: Consolidate Data

To consolidate data:

1. Open all the workbooks from which you want to consolidate data.
2. Arrange the windows in the desired position and size.
3. Select the worksheet and the cell or range of cells where you want the consolidated data to be placed.
4. On the Data tab, in the Data Tools section, click Consolidate.
5. In the Consolidate dialog box, from the Function drop-down list, select a built-in function to consolidate data, if desired.
6. In the Reference text box, enter the cell reference for the range of data you want to consolidate from the other worksheets.
7. Click Add to add the specified reference to the All References section.
8. In necessary, add more references to the All References section.
9. Check the Create Links To Source Data check box to create a link to the source data.
10. Click OK to complete the consolidation.

ACTIVITY 5-2
Consolidating Data

Data Files:

Hanover.xlsx, Monder.xlsx, Jaen.xlsx, Consolidation.xlsx

Before You Begin:

From C:\084892Data\Working with Multiple Workbooks, open Hanover.xlsx, Monder.xlsx, Jaen.xlsx, and Consolidation.xlsx.

Scenario:

You have three sales reports (Hanover, Monder, and Jaen) that need to be summarized. You need to consolidate the data in the Consolidation workbook. You will consolidate the range that contains the quantity data on each of the worksheets in the consolidation worksheet.

What You Do	How You Do It
1. In the Consolidation workbook, select the range where you want the consolidated data to be placed.	a. On the View tab, in the Window group, **click Arrange All.**
	b. In the Arrange Windows dialog box, in the Arrange section, **select Tiled and click OK.**
	c. **Double-click the title bar of the Consolidation.xlsx window** to maximize it.
	d. **Select the range C5:C14** to select the cells that will hold the quantity data.

2. **Reference the range that has the quantity data from the Monder workbook.**

   a. On the Data tab, in the Data Tools group, **click Consolidate.**

   b. In the Consolidate dialog box, next to the Reference text box, **click the Collapse Dialog button.** 🔳

   c. On the View tab, in the Window group, **click Switch Windows and select Monder.xlsx.**

   d. **Select the range C5:C14** to select the quantity data and **press Enter.**

   e. In the Consolidate dialog box, **click Add** to add the specified reference to the All References list box.

3. **Reference the range that has the quantity data from the Jaen workbook and the Hanover workbook.**

   a. In the Consolidate dialog box, **click the Collapse Dialog button.**

   b. In the Window group, **click Switch Windows and select Jaen.xlsx.**

   c. **Select the range C5:C14** to select the quantity data and **press Enter.**

   d. In the Consolidate dialog box, **click Add** to add the specified reference to the All References list box.

   e. **Reference the range that has the quantity data from Hanover.xlsx.**

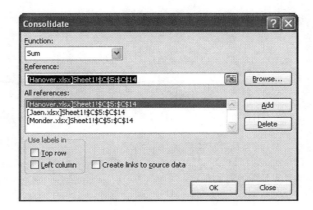

4. **Create links to the source data.**

   a. **Check the Create Links To Source Data check box.**

   b. **Click OK** to complete the consolidation.

c. In the consolidated workbook, notice that the quantity data from all the workbooks has been consolidated.

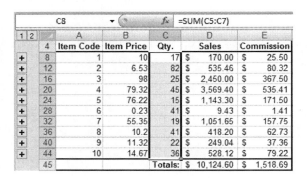

5. **View the hidden data in the consolidated workbook.**

a. Below the Name box, **click 2** to expand all of the hidden data.

b. **Click cell C5.**

c. In the Formula bar, notice that the data is from Hanover.xlsx.

d. **Click cell C6.**

e. In the Formula bar, notice that the data is from Jaen.xlsx.

f. **Click cell C7.**

g. In the Formula bar, notice that the data is from Monder.xlsx.

h. **Save Consolidation.xlsx as *My Consolidation.xlsx* and close all open files.**

TOPIC C

Link Cells in Different Workbooks

You have consolidated data into a single worksheet. Now you would like to connect the data stored in one workbook to the data in another workbook. In this topic, you will link cells in different workbooks.

You have five different, but related, workbooks. Currently you have to open each one separately when you need to work on their content. However, because the data is related, you believe it would be more efficient to create a direct link from one cell in one workbook to another related cell in a different workbook. You can do this by linking the cells in the different workbooks. Linking cells in different workbooks can smooth your workflow by removing the need to open workbooks that contain related data.

How to Link Cells in Different Workbooks

Procedure Reference: Link Cells in Different Workbooks

To link cells in different workbooks:

1. Open the workbook that will contain the links and the workbooks to which you will link.
2. In the workbook that will contain the links, select the cell where you want to place the formula that will contain the links, and then begin creating a formula.
3. Select the cells in the other workbooks that contain the data you want to link to using operators as needed to create the formula.
4. Press Enter when you have finished creating the formula.

External References

An *external reference* is a reference to another workbook or to a defined name in another workbook.

Source and Dependent Workbooks

A *source workbook* is the workbook to which a formula refers, and a *dependent workbook* is a workbook that contains a link to another workbook.

ACTIVITY 5-3
Linking Cells in Different Workbooks

Data Files:

Finch.xlsx, Decker.xlsx, Weckl.xlsx, Summary.xlsx

Before You Begin:

From C:\084892Data\Working with Multiple Workbooks, open Finch.xlsx, Decker.xlsx, Weckl.xlsx, and Summary.xlsx.

Scenario:

You need to calculate the total sales and total commission for the three sales representatives whose data is stored in the Finch, Decker, and Weckl workbooks, respectively. You have already begun developing the Summary workbook that will summarize and calculate the total for each of the files. Any update to the sales data in any of the files should be reflected in the Summary workbook.

What You Do	How You Do It
1. **Create a formula that sums the sales totals from each of the sales representatives' worksheets.**	a. **Tile the windows.**
	b. **Activate the Summary.xlsx window.**
	c. **Click cell A5 and type** = to begin creating the formula.
	d. **Activate the Finch.xlsx window.**
	e. In the Finch.xlsx window, **scroll down and click cell D15.**
	f. **Type** + to continue keying in the formula.
	g. **Activate the Decker.xlsx window.**
	h. In the Decker.xlsx window, **scroll down, click cell D15, and type** +
	i. **Activate the Weckl.xlsx window.**
	j. In the Weckl.xlsx window, **scroll down, click cell D15, and press Enter.**
	k. Notice that the value of Total Sales displayed in cell A5 of Summary.xlsx is $10,124.60.

2. **Update the sales data for Item 3 in Finch.xlsx.**

a. **Activate the Finch.xlsx workbook.**

b. In the Finch.xlsx window, **click cell D7 and press Delete.**

c. **Type *200* and press Enter.**

d. Notice that the Total Sales value in Summary.xlsx changes to $9,148.60.

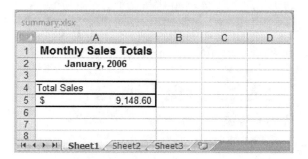

e. **Save the Summary and Finch workbooks with the prefix "My" and close all the other files.**

TOPIC D
Edit Links

You have created links between different workbooks. You now need to change the reference to a linked cell in a source workbook. In this topic, you will edit links.

You have a workbook which contains links to the cells in another workbook. However, the cells that contain the data you are linking to in the source workbook have moved. Rather than creating a new link from scratch, you decide to edit the existing link so that it directs you to the correct destination cell. Editing links can minimize upkeep time because you don't have to create a new link from scratch.

How to Edit Links

Procedure Reference: Edit Links

To edit links:

1. Open the file that contains the links you want to edit.
2. On the message bar, click Options.
3. In the Microsoft Office Security Options dialog box, select the Enable This Content option and click OK to allow the update of the link.
4. In the Microsoft Office Excel warning box, click Edit Links.
5. In the Edit Links dialog box, select the name of the workbook with the link to be redirected.
6. Click Change Source.
7. In the Change Source: [Filename] dialog box, select the name of the workbook to which you want to establish a new link.
8. Click OK to change the source file.
9. In the Edit Links dialog box, click Close.

ACTIVITY 5-4

Editing Links

Data Files:

Weckl.xlsx

Before You Begin:

From C:\084892Data\Working with Multiple Workbooks, open Weckl.xlsx and maximize the workbook.

Scenario:

Janet Weckl has changed her name to Janet Covington. Her workbook has to be edited and renamed to reflect this change. Additionally, you need to ensure that the link in the My Summary workbook that currently addresses the Weckl workbook will point to the new Covington workbook you will create.

What You Do	How You Do It
1. **Edit the Weckl workbook to reflect Ms. Covington's name change.**	a. **Click cell D1 and press Delete.**
	b. **Type** *Janet Covington* **and press Enter.**
	c. **Save and close the file.**
	d. In Windows Explorer, **navigate to C:\084892Data\Working with Multiple Workbooks and rename the Weckl file to** *Covington.xlsx*
	e. **Close Windows Explorer.**

2. **Edit the My Summary workbook so that it points to the Covington workbook.**

a. From the C:\084892Data\Working with Multiple Workbooks folder, **open My Summary.xlsx.**

b. On the message bar below the Ribbon, **click Options.**

c. In the Microsoft Office Security Options dialog box, **select the Enable This Content option and click OK** to allow the update of the link.

d. In the Microsoft Office Excel warning box, **click Edit Links.**

e. Observe that the status of Weckl.xlsx is displayed as Error: Source Not Found.

f. In the Edit Links dialog box, in the list box, **select Weckl.xlsx.**

g. **Click Change Source.**

h. In the Change Source: Weckl.xlsx dialog box, **select Covington.xlsx and click OK** to change the source file.

i. In the Edit Links dialog box, notice that the status of the file has changed to OK.

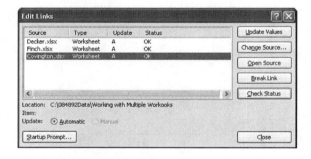

j. In the Edit Links dialog box, **click Close.**

k. **Save the file as *My Updated Summary.xlsx* and close it.**

Lesson 5 Follow-up

In this lesson, you worked with multiple workbooks. You also learned that you can use a single Excel file as a repository for data from multiple workbooks.

1. **What data are you currently working with that would benefit from consolidation? If you are not currently working on a project that could benefit from data consolidation, how might you deploy data consolidation in future projects?**

2. **How might you deploy workspaces in your organization?**

6 | Importing and Exporting Data

Lesson Time: 30 minutes

Lesson Objectives:

In this lesson, you will import and export data.

You will:

- Export Excel data.
- Import a delimited text file.

Introduction

You shared data between different worksheets and workbooks. You would now like to begin sharing Microsoft® Office Excel® data with other applications. In this lesson, you will import and export data from Excel to other applications.

Re-creating data in one application when you have already created that data in another can be cumbersome and requires a lot of extra effort. Importing and exporting data allows you to use data from other applications in Excel and vice versa without having to re-create it from scratch.

TOPIC A

Export Excel Data

You have consolidated and created workbooks that contain links to other workbooks. You would now like to use some of the data stored in an Excel file in other applications. In this topic, you will export Excel worksheet data.

Imagine you have created a worksheet that tracks warehouse orders. You are using Microsoft Word to create a small brochure you plan to distribute at an upcoming seminar, and you want to include some of the data from the warehouse order worksheet in the brochure. Rather than recreating the data you have already created in Excel, you can export the data from Excel to Word. Exporting data from Excel to other applications will minimize your effort and save time.

File Export

Definition:

File export is a method of sending data that has been created in one application to a different application. When data is exported, a copy of the data is formatted specifically for the application it will be used in, and the original data stays the same. The data exported can be manipulated in the new application. Excel can export a range of data, a worksheet, or an entire workbook.

Example:

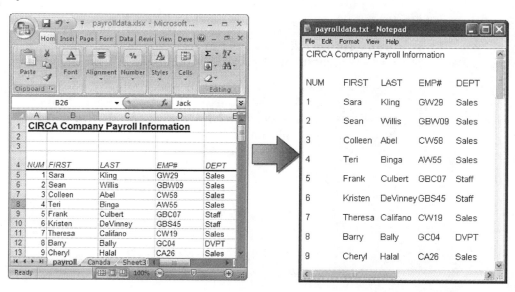

Data in Excel   Data after exporting to Notepad

File Types for Exporting Excel Data

Excel data can be exported in a variety of file types. The file type is determined by the application to which you are exporting the data.

File Type	Description
XML	Saves a workbook as an eXtensible Markup Language file. Primarily, web-based applications make use of this format.
HTML	Saves a workbook as a HyperText Markup Language. Data being used on the web or viewed in a web browser is saved in this format. Using this file type, you can save the entire workbook or the active worksheet alone.
TXT	Saves a workbook as a tab-delimited text file for word processing. This file type does not allow you to save multiple sheets as does the HTML file type. It saves only the active sheet.
CSV	Saves a workbook as a comma-delimited text file.

Exporting Excel Files to Word

In Excel 2007, there is no option for exporting an Excel file as a Word document directly. Therefore, you will save Excel files in the TXT file format and then process them in Word.

How to Export Excel Data

Procedure Reference: Save Excel Data in a Different File Format

To save Excel data in a different file format:

1. With a workbook open, display the Save As dialog box.
2. If necessary, from the Save In drop-down list, select the location to save the file.
3. In the File Name text box, enter the name of the file.
4. From the Save As Type drop-down list, select the desired file format, and then click Save.

Procedure Reference: Export Excel Data to Use in Microsoft Word

To export Excel data to use in Microsoft Word:

1. Open the worksheet that needs to be exported to Word.
2. Display the Save As dialog box.
3. From the Save In drop-down list, select the location for the new file.
4. In the File Name text box, enter a desired name.
5. From the Save As Type drop-down list, select Text (Tab Delimited)(*.txt).
6. In the Microsoft Office Excel warning box, click Save to save only the active worksheet.
7. In the Microsoft Office Excel information box, click Yes to leave out any incompatible features.
8. If necessary, open the TXT file in Microsoft Office Word.

ACTIVITY 6-1

Exporting Excel Data to Use in Microsoft Word

Data Files:

Payroll Data.xlsx

Before You Begin:

From C:\084892Data\Importing and Exporting Data, open Payroll Data.xlsx.

Scenario:

Your manager has signed off on the data contained in the Payroll Data workbook. Now you need to make this data available in Word so that you can use the application's mail merge feature to distribute payroll information to all the employees listed in the Payroll Data workbook.

What You Do	How You Do It
1. Save the Payroll worksheet as a tab delimited text file.	a. **Select the Payroll worksheet tab.**
	b. **Display the Save As dialog box.**
	c. In the File Name text box, **type *My Payroll Data***
	d. From the Save As Type drop-down list, **select Text (Tab Delimited) (*.txt).**
	e. **Click Save.**
	f. In the Microsoft Office Excel warning box, **click OK** to save only the active worksheet.
	g. In the Microsoft Office Excel message box, **click Yes** to retain the existing format and leave out any incompatible features.
	h. **Close the workbook without saving it.**
2. View the content of Payroll Data.txt in Word.	a. **Choose Start→All Programs→Microsoft Office→Microsoft Office Word 2007.**
	b. **Click the Office button and choose Open.**
	c. **Navigate to C:\084892Data\Importing and Exporting Data.**

d. If necessary, from the Files Of Type drop-down list, **select All Files (*.*).**

e. **Select My Payroll Data.txt and click Open.**

f. Notice that the data exported from Excel is open in the Word document.

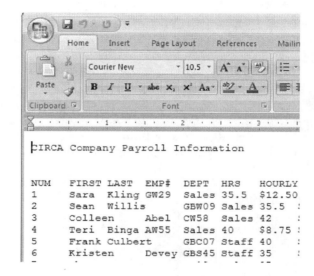

g. **Display the Save As dialog box.**

h. In the File Name text box, **type *My Payroll Data***

i. From the Save As Type drop-down list, **select Word Document (*.docx).**

j. **Click Save** to save the text file as a Word document.

k. **Close the file and close Word.**

TOPIC B

Import a Delimited Text File

You have imported data from Microsoft Word. You now have a text file that contains data, delimited by tabs, that you need to split and display in different columns. In this topic, you will import data from a delimited text file to Excel.

When you have a text file that contains numerical data separated by tabs or commas that needs to be formatted and have calculations run on it, it would be easier to split data into different columns. This would allow you to work more proficiently and comfortably. By importing delimited text files into Excel, you can split data to different columns, thereby giving you the flexibility to format and manipulate data with Excel's toolset.

File Import

Definition:

File import is a method of capturing data from one application for use in another application. Excel can import all the data or selected data from a file. The import changes the data format so that it can be manipulated within a worksheet. The imported data appears no different from data that has been created directly in Excel and can be manipulated in the same manner. The data can be imported from other spreadsheet applications, databases, text documents, or the web.

Example:

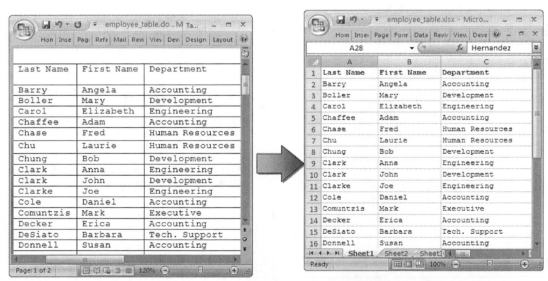

Table in a Word document   Table after importing to an Excel
                                            worksheet

The Get External Data Group

The Get External Data group on the Data tab contains commands that will allow you to import data from other applications into Excel.

Command	Description
From Access	Imports external data from an Access database.
From Web	Imports external data from the web.
From Text	Imports external data from a text file.
From Other Sources	Imports data from other sources such as SQL Server, Analysis Services, XML Data Import, Data Connection Wizard, and Microsoft Query.
Existing Connections	Imports external data from an existing connection. This command opens the Existing Connections dialog box which allows you to select a data source from the list of commonly used data sources.

Delimited Text Files

Definition:

A *delimited text file* is a TXT file that contains data fields separated or delimited by certain characters. Tab is the default character to delimit data in TXT files, but this character can also be changed to commas, quotation marks, or spaces. Delimited text files can be created in most word processing applications.

Example:

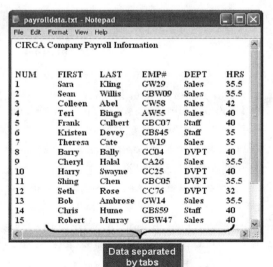

Methods of Importing Text Files

In Excel, you can import data from a text file in two different ways. The text file can either be opened directly in Excel or imported as an external data range. While directly opening in Excel, you do not establish a connection to the text file, whereas by specifying the data in the text file as external data to import, you will establish a connection to the text file. Any changes made to the original text file will be reflected in the corresponding data in the worksheet whenever it is refreshed.

How to Import a Delimited Text File

Procedure Reference: Import a Delimited Text File by Opening It

To import a delimited text file by opening it:

1. Open a new or existing Excel worksheet into which you want to import the text file and select the cell in which the text file will start when imported.

2. Display the Open dialog box.

3. Select the delimited text file you want to import into Excel and click Open.

4. On the Text Import Wizard - Step 1 Of 3 page, in the Preview Of File section, set the desired options, preview the selected data to be split, and click Next.

5. On the Text Import Wizard- Step 2 Of 3 page, in the Delimiters section, check or uncheck the desired delimiter check boxes.

6. If necessary, check the Treat Consecutive Delimiters As One check box to avoid the creation of an extra column if there are two subsequent delimiters.

7. If necessary, from the Text Qualifier drop-down list, select the desired option.

    *   Select " (quotation mark) to specify that the delimiter within any text between quotation marks should be ignored.

    *   Select ' (apostrophe) to specify that the delimiter within any text that follows an apostrophe should be ignored.

    *   Or, select None to ignore text qualifiers.

8. In the Data Preview section, preview the split contents and click Next.

9. On the Text Import Wizard - Step 3 Of 3 page, in the Data Preview section, select the desired column and then select a column data format option in order to specify the type of data for the content to be split.

    *   Select the General option in order to convert all currency number characters to the Excel currency format.

    *   Select the Text option in order to convert all number characters to the Excel text format.

    *   Select the Date option and, from the Date drop-down list, select the desired date format, to convert all date characters to the Excel date format.

    *   Or, select the Do Not Import Column (Skip) option in order to avoid splitting and moving the column selected in the preview section.

 You need to choose the data format that closely matches the preview data.

10. If necessary, click Advanced and, in the Advanced Text Import Settings dialog box, specify the settings used to recognize numeric data and click OK.

11. Click Finish.

12. If necessary, format the imported data in the worksheet as required.

Procedure Reference: Import a Text File by Connecting to It

To import a text file by connecting to it:

1. Open a new or existing Excel worksheet into which you want to import the text file.

2. On the Data tab, in the Get External Data group, click From Text.

3. In the Import Text File dialog box, navigate to the delimited text file and click Import.

4. In the Text Import Wizard, specify the settings to import the delimited file.

5. Click Finish.

6. If necessary, in the Import Data dialog box, specify the location for the import.

    ● Choose Existing Worksheet and specify the location in the text box to place the import in the active worksheet.

    ● Or, choose New Worksheet to place the import in a new worksheet, starting at cell A1.

7. In the Import Data dialog box, click Properties.

8. In the External Data Range dialog box, in the Refresh Control section, set the refresh properties.

    ● Check the Prompt For File Name On Refresh check box to prompt for the file name on every refresh.

    ● Check the Refresh Every check box and specify the time period in the minutes list box, to refresh the data in the imported file in every specified time gap.

    ● Or, check the Refresh Data When Opening The File check box to refresh data whenever the file is opened.

9. In the Import Data dialog box, click OK.

10. If necessary, format the worksheet as required.

ACTIVITY 6-2

Importing a Delimited Text File

Data Files:

Payroll.txt

Before You Begin:

Open a new workbook in Excel.

Scenario:

The Payroll text file is a comma-delimited text file which contains the employee payroll data. You have been tasked with converting the comma-delimited file into an Excel file so that the employee payroll data can, going forward, be stored in Excel and can reflect all the changes made to the text file every time the text file is updated.

What You Do	How You Do It
1. **Select the Payroll text file to import into Excel.**	a. On the Data tab, in the Get External Data group, **click From Text.**
	b. In the Import Text File dialog box, **navigate to C:\084892Data\Importing and Exporting Data.**
	c. **Select Payroll.txt and click Import.**
2. **Specify the delimiter settings for the text to be imported.**	a. On the Text Import Wizard - Step 1 Of 3 page, **click Next** to accept delimited as the data file type and to start the import at row 1.
	b. On the Text Import Wizard - Step 2 Of 3 page, in the Delimiters section, **uncheck the Tab check box, check the Comma check box, and click Next.**
	c. On the Text Import Wizard - Step 3 Of 3 page, **verify that General is selected as the Column Data format and click Finish.**

3. Set the import properties for the delimited text.	a. In the Import Data dialog box, **click Properties.**
	b. In the External Data Range Properties dialog box, in the Refresh Control section, **check the Refresh Data When Opening The File check box and click OK** to refresh data in the imported file whenever it is opened.
	c. In the Import Data dialog box, **click OK** to import data to the existing worksheet.
	d. Notice that the delimited text has been imported to the Excel worksheet.

e. **Save the file as *My Payroll Import.xlsx* close it.**

Lesson 6 Follow-up

In this lesson, you imported and exported data between Excel and other applications. By importing and exporting data, you can use data from other applications in Excel and Excel data in other applications without having to re-create it from scratch.

1. **While using Excel, what type of data would you like to import from other applications? Why?**

2. **Consider a project for which you are currently using Excel. How would the data layout or structure benefit if you exported that data to Microsoft Office Word?**

7 | Using Excel with the Web

Lesson Time: 20 minutes

Lesson Objectives:

In this lesson, you will use Excel with the web.

You will:

- Publish a worksheet to the web.
- Import data from the web.
- Create a web query to import dynamic data from the web.

Introduction

You exported and imported Microsoft® Office Excel® worksheets to other applications. You now want to incorporate data from the web into workbooks and make them available to other individuals via the web. In this lesson, you will import data from the web into a workbook and export your workbooks to the web.

While creating a workbook, you might want to add additional information from the web to your workbook or you may want others to access your workbook from anywhere. When you export data to the web, you can view and change Excel files on any computer with an Internet connection, without the Excel application. When you import data from the web, you can incorporate the necessary information into a workbook. Even better, the data will automatically update in your workbook when the information on the web is updated.

TOPIC A

Publish a Worksheet to the Web

You have exported and imported Excel worksheets to and from other applications. Now, you want to access and manipulate a worksheet you created on your hard drive, from another computer over the Internet by publishing it to the web. In this topic, you will publish an Excel worksheet to the web.

Wouldn't it be convenient if you could view, manipulate, and make changes to workbooks that you created on your computer from anywhere and any computer? Excel allows you to do just that. By publishing worksheets to the web, you can enhance the reach of your worksheet and make it more accessible.

File Publish

Definition:

File publish is a method of publishing data that has been created in an application to a web page. The data in the published file can be manipulated from any computer that has access to the web. Excel can publish a range of data, a worksheet, or an entire workbook to the web.

Example:

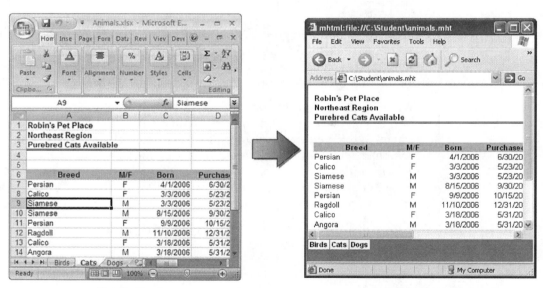

Data in Excel
worksheet

Excel worksheet data
published as a web page

The Publish As Web Page Dialog Box

The Publish As Web Page dialog box allows you to transform Excel data into a web page that can be uploaded to a web server. This dialog box contains various options to publish Excel data to a web page.

Option	Description
Choose	Allows you to specify whether it is the entire workbook, a single worksheet, or a range of cells that need to be published as a web page. The previously published items in the workbook will be listed in the list box below.
Title	Displays the title of the web page.
Change	Launches the Set Title dialog box where you can specify a name for the web page.
File Name	Displays the location specified for the web page and also allows you to type a new location for the web page.
Browse	Launches the Publish As dialog box where you can browse through your computer and specify the location and name for your web page.
AutoRepublish Every Time This Workbook Is Saved	Allows you to autorepublish your workbook every time it is saved.
Open Published Web Page In Browser	Allows you to open the published web page in a browser.
Publish	Publishes the selected Excel data as a web page.

Publishing a Range of Cells

When you have to publish a range of cells as a web page, you can specify the desired range in the list box below the Choose drop-down list in the Publish As Web Page dialog box.

Publishing a Web Page

Publishing is one way to generate the HTML format that is required to display information on the web. When you publish a web page, you have more options than when you simply export the data in an HTML format. While the data that is published as a web page can be manipulated through any web browser, exported HTML data cannot be manipulated likewise.

How to Publish a Worksheet to the Web

Procedure Reference: Publish a Worksheet to the Web

To publish a worksheet to the web:

1. In the Save As dialog box, select a location in which you need to save the web page.

2. In the File Name text box, type a file name.

3. From the Save As Type drop-down list, select an option in order to save the worksheet as a web page.

   - Select Single File Web Page (*.mht; *.mhtml) to save the worksheet as a web page that includes all the supporting information.

   - Or, select Web Page (*.htm; *.html) to save the worksheet as a web page and also to create a folder that contains all the supporting information.

4. If necessary, add a title for the web page.

   a. Click Change Title.

   b. In the Set Page Title dialog box, in the Page Title text box, type a title for the page and click OK.

5. In the Save As dialog box, click Publish.

6. In the Publish As Web Page dialog box, set publication properties.

   a. In the Item To Publish section, from the Choose drop-down list, select the item to be published.

   b. If necessary, click Change, and in the Set Title dialog box, specify a different name for the page and click OK.

   c. Click Browse, and in the Publish As dialog box, specify the desired location and a name to publish the web page.

   d. Check the AutoRepublish Every Time This Workbook Is Saved check box to autorepublish the workbook every time it is saved.

   e. If necessary, check the Open Published Web Page In Browser check box to open the published web page in a browser.

7. Click Publish to publish the presentation as a web page.

ACTIVITY 7-1

Publishing a Worksheet to the Web

Data Files:

Animals.xlsx

Before You Begin:

From C:\084892Data\Using Excel with the Web, open Animals.xlsx.

Scenario:

For some reason, at Robin's Pet Place, cats don't seem to be selling as fast as the other animals. The owner has decided to have the Cats worksheet in the Animals workbook available on the Internet to see if that will generate more sales. She also wants the web page to reflect any and all changes she makes in the Animals workbook every time she saves it, so that the latest information is always available on the Internet. She has decided to name the web page Robin's Pet Place – Purebred Cats Available, and name the file My Cats Page.

What You Do	How You Do It
1. **Specify a file name for the Cats worksheet to be saved as a web page.**	a. In the Save As dialog box, in the File Name text box, **triple click and type *My Cats Page***
	b. From the Save As Type drop-down list, **select Single File Web Page (*.mht; *.mhtml).**
2. **Set a title for the web page.**	a. **Click Change Title.**
	b. In the Set Page Title dialog box, in the Page Title text box, **type *Robin's Pet Place – Purebred Cats Available* and click OK.**

3. Publish the Cats worksheet as a web page.

a. In the Save As dialog box, **click Publish.**

b. In the Publish As Web Page dialog box, in the Item To Publish section, from the Choose drop-down list, **select Items On Cats.**

c. In the Publish As section, **check the AutoRepublish Every Time This Workbook Is Saved check box.**

d. **Check the Open Published Web Page In Browser check box and click Publish.**

e. Notice that the worksheet opens in a browser window.

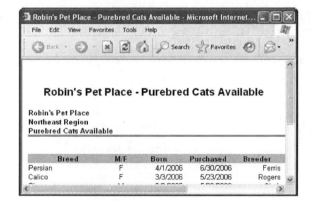

f. **Close the browser window.**

g. **Close the workbook without saving.**

TOPIC B
Import Data from the Web

You published your worksheet as a web page, thereby enhancing the reach of your worksheet. Now, you would like to use data that you found on the web in your workbook. In this topic, you will import data from the web to your workbook.

When you are browsing the web, you might find data that you would like to use in your workbook. You could cut and paste the data, but it would be a very tedious process and there is no guarantee that it would copy correctly. You might even miss some of the data altogether. In order to capture data from the web, you can import the data and be sure you get exactly the data you wanted.

How to Import Data from the Web

Procedure Reference: Import Data from the Web

To import data from the web:

1. With the desired worksheet open, on the Data tab, in the Get External Data group, click Existing Connections.

2. In the Existing Connections dialog box, from the Show drop-down list, select a connection option.

    ●   Select All Connections to display all the connection files available.

    ●   Select Connections In This Workbook to display all files connected to the active workbook.

    ●   Select Connection Files On The Network to display all files connected to the network.

    ●   Or, select Connection Files On This Computer to display all files connected to this computer.

3. In the Select A Connection list box, select the desired file connection and click Open.

4. If necessary, in the Import Data dialog box, select where you would like to put the data.

5. If necessary, in the Import Data dialog box, click Properties, set the refresh properties, and click OK.

6. Click OK to import the data to the worksheet.

ACTIVITY 7-2

Importing Data from the Web

Data Files:

Currency Rates.xlsx

Before You Begin:

From C:\084892Data\Using Excel with the Web, open Currency Rates.xlsx.

Scenario:

The President of Robin's Pet Place is considering doing business in other countries. She asked you to download information from the web on currency rates to a new workbook so that she can review them.

What You Do	How You Do It
1. **Open the currency rate information to be imported from the web into the Currency Rates workbook.**	a. On the Data tab, in the Get External Data group, **click Existing Connections.**
	b. In the Existing Connections dialog box, in the Select A Connection list box, observe that MSN MoneyCentral Investor Currency Rates is selected by default and **click Open.**

2. Import the currency rate information.

a. In the Import Data dialog box, **click OK** to accept cell A3 as the default location in the existing worksheet and to start the import.

b. Observe that the selected data is imported into the worksheet.

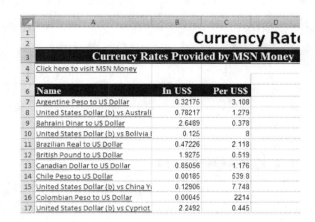

	A	B	C	D
1				
2		**Currency Rate**		
3	**Currency Rates Provided by MSN Money**			
4	Click here to visit MSN Money			
5				
6	**Name**	**In US$**	**Per US$**	
7	Argentine Peso to US Dollar	0.32175	3.108	
8	United States Dollar (b) vs Australi	0.78217	1.279	
9	Bahraini Dinar to US Dollar	2.6489	0.378	
10	United States Dollar (b) vs Bolivia	0.125	8	
11	Brazilian Real to US Dollar	0.47226	2.118	
12	British Pound to US Dollar	1.9275	0.519	
13	Canadian Dollar to US Dollar	0.85056	1.176	
14	Chile Peso to US Dollar	0.00185	539.8	
15	United States Dollar (b) vs China Y	0.12906	7.748	
16	Colombian Peso to US Dollar	0.00045	2214	
17	United States Dollar (b) vs Cypriot	2.2492	0.445	

c. **Save the workbook as *My Currency Rates.xlsx* and close it**.

TOPIC C
Create a Web Query

You have imported data that always stays the same, from the web into your workbook. You now need to import data that changes on a regular basis into your workbook, as and when changes are made to the data on the web page. In this topic, you will create a web query to import dynamic data from the web.

There is a large amount of data on the web that changes on a daily, sometimes hourly, basis. Capturing this data by importing it would require repeating the import process over and over again, and you could never really be sure that the data was current. Fortunately, in Excel, you can create a web query that will update the data you import without requiring your intervention.

Web Queries

A web query allows you to import data that changes frequently on the web. It determines what portions of the web page are available to import. A web query can be used to import a single table, multiple tables, or all of the text on a web page. Unlike other imported data, web query data is updated in the worksheet automatically each time the information on the website is updated. A connection to the Internet is necessary for the data to update.

The New Web Query Dialog Box

The New Web Query dialog box contains various options that will allow you to import data from the web by creating a query.

Option	Description
Address	Allows you to enter the URL of the web page from where you need to import data.
Go	Allows you to go to the specified URL.
Back	Allows you to go to the previous page visited.
Forward	Allows you to go to the next page.
Stop	Allows you to stop the search for the web page specified in the Address text box.
Refresh	Allows you to refresh the active web page.
Hide Icons/Show Icons	Allows you to toggle between the hide and show options that will allow you to select the tables to be imported from the web page.
Save Query	Opens the Save Query dialog box, which will allow you to specify the location and name for the query, and save the query file.
Options	Opens the Web Query Options dialog box, which will allow you to adjust the way Excel imports the data.
Web page area	Displays the web page chosen. Breaks data into groups that are generally referred to as tables and are marked by small yellow boxes. You can select the table or tables and import them into Excel.

Option	Description
Import	Allows you to import the selected data from the web into Excel. This button will display the Import Data dialog box, where you can specify the location for the imported data.
Cancel	Allows you to cancel import.

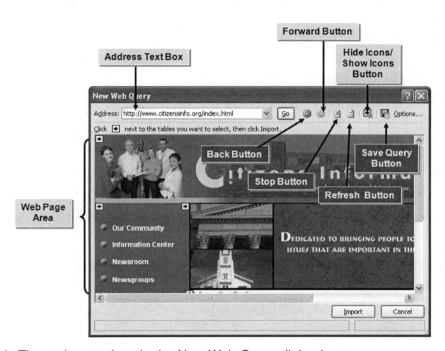

Figure 7-1: *The various options in the New Web Query dialog box.*

Data in the New Web Query Dialog Box

In the New Web Query dialog box, you can navigate to the desired web page and select the table or tables of information that you want to import into Excel. Data on a web page is broken into groups that are generally referred to as tables. These groups are marked by small yellow boxes with arrows that appear at the top left of each table of information. You can select a table of information by clicking this box and after selection the box changes to green with a check mark. On clicking the box again, the table becomes deselected.

How to Create a Web Query

Procedure Reference: Create a Web Query

To create a web query:

1. Select the worksheet to which the data will be imported.

2. On the Data tab, in the Get External data group, click From Web.

3. In the New Web Query dialog box, navigate to the web page from where you want to import data.

   a. In the Address text box, type the URL of the web page from where you need to import data.

   b. Click Go.

4. On the web page displayed in the New Web Query dialog box, select the table you want to import and click Import.

5. In the Import Data dialog box, if necessary, select where you would like to put the data and set the refresh properties.

6. Click OK.

DISCOVERY ACTIVITY 7-3
Identifying How to Create a Web Query

Scenario:

You have been tracking new video release dates, and the most popular movies on DVD, by analyzing consumer rating on several websites. You need to compile the current data available into a spreadsheet for potential investors and keep the information current for future meetings.

1. **Which option allows you to determine the portions of a web page that are available for import?**

    a) A specific type of website.

    b) A specific format.

    c) The web administrator.

    d) The web query.

2. **True or False? The data inserted into a worksheet using a web query is updated automatically.**

    ___ True

    ___ False

3. **Which option in the Get External Data group of the Data tab allows you to open the New Web Query dialog box to import data from the web to your Excel worksheet?**

    a) From Other Sources

    b) From Web

    c) Existing Connections

    d) From Text

4. **Which option in the New Web Query dialog box will allow you to adjust the way Excel imports data from the web?**

    a) Save Query

    b) Hide Icons / Show Icons

    c) Options

    d) Web page area

Lesson 7 Follow-up

In this lesson, you used Excel with the web. Whether you need to transfer workbook data to the web for others to see, or import data from the web, so that you can work within a worksheet, working with data on the web offers flexibility and portability for your data.

1. **What type of data do you work with that might be useful to export?**

2. **What type of data would you import?**

8 | Structuring Workbooks with XML

Lesson Time: 25 minutes

Lesson Objectives:

In this lesson, you will structure workbooks with XML.

You will:

- Develop XML maps.
- Import and export XML data.

Introduction

You have imported static and dynamic data from the web into Microsoft® Office Excel®. You would now like to exchange your Excel data with other applications while meeting emerging standards for data storage and distribution. In this lesson, you will structure workbooks with XML.

Your workbook contains data that managers need to access via print and the web. When you use Excel's standard import and export tools on the data in the worksheet as it is, the print and web versions do not fit in the layout of your existing brochure and website. Structuring workbooks with XML allows you to exchange data with other XML-compliant applications, thus enabling you to create data once and deliver it on multiple platforms in various visual layouts.

TOPIC A

Develop XML Maps

You have imported dynamic and static data from the web to Excel. You would now like to manipulate some XML data in Excel. In this topic, you will develop XML maps to map contents of XML to Excel workbooks.

When you have data stored in an XML file that you want to manipulate using the Excel user interface, you need to have a way to get the data from the XML source into Excel, in such a way that the data appears in Excel in an easily readable and familiar format. XML maps relate the contents of an XML data source to specified ranges in an Excel workbook so that the data from the XML source appears in a visually structured, Excel-style layout.

XML

Definition:

XML, or eXtensible Markup Language, is a language that describes data by creating structured text files that are readable and easy to interpret. XML elements contain tags and the data within the tags. Once defined, the data can be exchanged between different systems or programs. XML files are saved with the .xml file extension. XML can be processed by a variety of databases and applications.

Example:

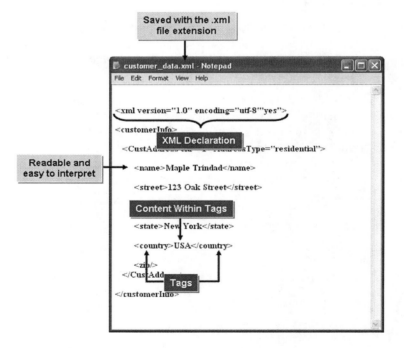

XML Components

An XML file has various components.

Component	Description
Opening tag	Begin with a less-than symbol, followed by the tag name, and then a greater than symbol.
Closing tag	Begin with a less-than symbol, followed by a forward slash, the tag name, and then a greater-than symbol.
Content	Everything that appears between the opening tag and the closing tag in an XML file.
Empty element	Begin with a less-than symbol, followed by the tag name and a space, and then a forward slash followed by a greater-than symbol.
Root element	Primary element in any XML file into which all other elements are nested.
Attribute	Additional data to describe the element included in the opening tag, after the element name.

The following figure identifies various XML components.

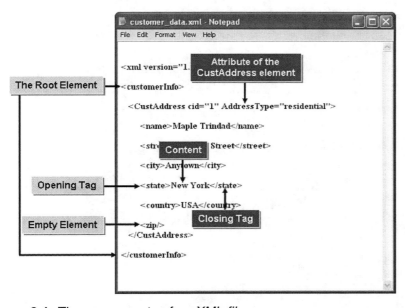

Figure 8-1: The components of an XML file.

Characteristics of XML Elements

The following characteristics apply to XML elements:

- Elements that contain content begin with an opening tag and end with a closing tag.
- Elements that do not contain content can use either opening and closing tags, or a single tag that defines the element as empty.
- Elements within other elements are called nested elements.
- Anything between the opening and closing tags of any given element is part of that element.
- Some elements can have attributes, which provide additional data to describe the element.

XML files must be well-formed. A well-formed document is the minimum structural requirement for XML documents to conform to. A well-formed XML document must have the following properties:

- Contain an XML declaration that identifies the file as an XML document.
- Contain a minimum of one element, the root element.
- Properly nest all elements within the root element.
- Properly nest all tags.
- Properly match start tags to corresponding end tags.
- Properly match tag names and the case of the tag name text for start tags and their corresponding end tags.

XML Schemas

Definition:

An *XML schema* is an XML file that sets rules and defines the structure of other XML files of a particular type. Schemas define the data type for the elements and attributes in XML files. Multiple XML files of the same type can use the same schema to validate their structure. XML schemas are saved with the .xsd file extension.

Example:

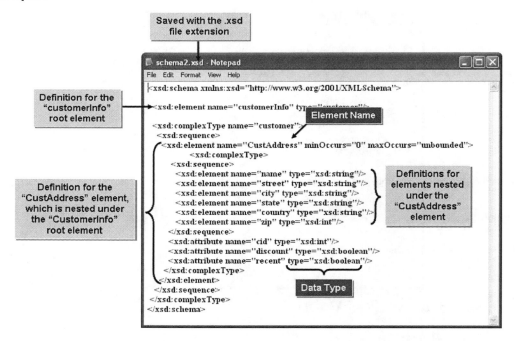

XML Maps

Definition:

An *XML map* is an Excel component that maps the contents of an Excel workbook to the corresponding elements and structure of a specified XML schema. After importing the necessary data, XML maps enable the export of the contents of the Excel workbook to any XML file that is of the type defined by the mapped XML schema. An XML map can apply some, or all, of the elements of a schema to a worksheet.

Example:

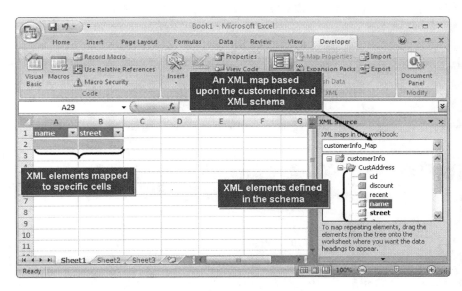

The XML Source Task Pane

The XML Source task pane contains various options that are used to manage XML maps.

Option	Description
XML Maps In This Workbook drop-down arrow	Displays a drop-down list that lists all the XML maps that have been added to the workbook. You can select the desired XML map from this list.
XML Maps In This Workbook list box	Lists the XML map and its elements that are selected from the XML Maps In This Workbook drop-down list.
Options button	Displays various options that will help you manage XML data.
XML Maps button	Opens the XML Maps dialog box that will allow you to add, delete, or rename XML maps.

The XML Group

The XML group on the Developer tab has various commands that will allow you to work with XML files in Excel, by mapping, importing, and exporting them.

Command	Allows You To
Source	Display the XML Source task pane, which will allow you to manage XML maps.
Map Properties	Modify or view XML map properties.
Expansion Packs	Create or manage XML expansion packs, the group of files that are created using an XML schema.
Refresh Data	Refresh the imported XML data in the workbook.
Import	Import an XML file.
Export	Export an XML file.

How to Develop XML Maps

Procedure Reference: Add an XML Map

To add an XML map:

1. Open the workbook to which you want to add the map or create a new blank workbook.
2. If necessary, customize the Ribbon to display the Developer tab.
   a. In the Excel Options dialog box, in the Change The Most Popular Options In Excel pane, in the Top Options For Working With Excel section, check the Show Developer Tab In The Ribbon check box, to display the Developer tab on the Ribbon.
   b. Click OK.
3. On the Developer tab, in the XML group, click Source.
4. In the XML Source task pane, click XML Maps.
5. In the XML Maps dialog box, click Add.
6. In the Select XML Source dialog box, navigate to the folder that contains the schema you need, select the schema, and then click Open to open the schema.
7. If necessary, click Add to add more maps to the current workbook.
8. In the XML Maps dialog box, click OK.
9. In the XML source task pane, drag the element to the desired location in the worksheet.

 You can also map the elements of an XML map to the worksheet by right-clicking the desired element. The Map Element option in the shortcut menu will display the Map XML Elements dialog box. You can specify the location for the new element in the Where Do You Want To Map The XML Elements text box.

Procedure Reference: Change the Location of XML Mapped Elements

To change the location of XML mapped elements:

1. Open the file that contains the XML map you want to modify.

2. On the worksheet, select a cell that has a mapped element.

3. Change the location of the selected element.

- Drag the selected cell to a new position in the workbook.

- Or, change the location using the XML Source task pane.

  a. In the XML Source task pane, right-click the highlighted XML element and choose Remove Element.

  b. In the XML Source task pane, right-click the highlighted XML element again and choose Map Element.

  c. In the Map XML dialog box, in the Where Do You Want To Map The XML Elements text box, specify the new location for the selected mapped element.

Procedure Reference: Delete an XML Map

To delete an XML map:

1. If necessary, open the file that contains the XML map you need to delete, and then open the XML Source task pane.

2. In the XML Source task pane, click XML Maps.

3. In the XML Maps dialog box, select the name of the map to delete and click Delete.

4. In the Microsoft Office Excel warning box, click OK so that you will no longer be able to import or export XML data using this map.

5. In the XML Maps dialog box, click OK.

ACTIVITY 8-1

Developing XML Maps

Data Files:

Schema1.xsd, Schema2.xsd

Before You Begin:

Open a new Excel workbook.

Scenario:

Your manager has sent you two XML schemas, Schema1 and Schema2. According to your manager, one of these files handles customer contact information; however, he doesn't know how to tell which file is which. Once you figure out which schema handles customer contact information, the other map can be deleted. You decide to view both schemas in Excel and then delete the map you are not going to use. You will then map the contents of the correct schema to an Excel sheet and name the workbook My New Customer Data.

What You Do	How You Do It
1. If necessary, display the Developer tab on the Ribbon.	a. In the Excel Options dialog box, in the Change The Most Popular Options In Excel pane, in the Top Options For Working With Excel section, check the Show Developer Tab In The Ribbon check box to display the Developer tab on the Ribbon.
	b. **Click OK.**

2. **Add Schema1.xsd and Schema2.xsd to a new, blank workbook.**

a. On the Developer tab, in the XML group, **click Source.**

b. In the XML Source task pane, **click XML Maps.**

c. In the XML Maps dialog box, **click Add.**

d. In the Select XML Source dialog box, **navigate to C:\084892Data\Structuring Workbooks with XML.**

e. **Select Schema1.xsd and click Open.**

f. In the XML Maps dialog box, **click Add.**

g. In the Select XML Source dialog box, **double-click Schema2.xsd** to add the schema to the XML Maps dialog box.

h. In the XML Maps dialog box, **click OK.**

i. Observe that customerInfo_Map listing the customer contact details is displayed in the XML Source task pane.

3. **Map customer contact information from the XML Source task pane to the worksheet.**

   a. From the XML Source task pane, **drag the Name element to cell A1.**

   b. From the XML Source task pane, **drag the Street element to cell A3.**

   c. From the XML Source task pane, **drag the City element to cell A5, the State element to cell A7, the Country element to cell A9, and then the Zip element to cell A11.**

4. **Modify the map you just created.**

   a. **Drag the Street element from cell A3 to cell B1.**

   b. **Drag the City element from cell A5 to cell C1.**

   c. **Drag the State element from cell A7 to cell D1, the Country element from cell A9 to cell E1, and then the Zip element from cell A11 to cell F1.**

5. **Delete the map that does not track customer contact information.**

   a. In the XML Source task pane, **click XML Maps.**

b. In the XML Maps dialog box, **select Listing_Map and click Delete.**

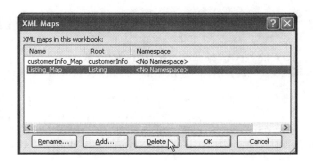

c. In the Microsoft Office Excel warning box, **click OK** so that you will no longer be able to export or import data using this XML map.

d. In the XML Maps dialog box, **click OK.**

e. On the Quick Access toolbar, **click the Save button.**

f. In the Save As dialog box, **navigate to C:\084892Data\Structuring Workbooks with XML.**

g. **Save the file as** *My New Customer Data*

TOPIC B
Import and Export XML Data

You have developed XML maps and now need to manipulate data stored in XML files using the Excel interface. In this topic, you will import and export XML data in Excel.

Being proficient in handling Excel files but not XML files, is absolutely not a cause for concern when you receive an XML file that you need to update with, include, or exclude data. You can access and manipulate the data using the Excel interface. Importing and exporting XML data allows you to manipulate data stored in XML files from within the Excel interface.

How to Import and Export XML Data

Procedure Reference: Import XML Data

To import XML data:

1. Open an existing workbook that has an XML map or create a new workbook.
2. If necessary, customize the Ribbon to display the Developer tab.
3. If necessary, map the elements of an XML schema to the workbook.
4. On the Developer tab, in the XML group, click Import.
5. In the Import XML dialog box, navigate to and select the file to be imported.
6. Click Import.

XML Import

If you are importing XML data into an Excel workbook and it is not already mapped to Excel through a schema, then Microsoft Office Excel will create a schema based on the XML data source. When data is imported as an XML table into the worksheet, the schema of the XML data file will be displayed in the XML Source task pane.

Procedure Reference: Import XML Data as External Data

To import XML data as an external data:

1. Open a new Excel workbook.
2. On the Data tab, in the Get External Data group, click From Other Sources and select From XML Data Import.
3. In the Select Data Source dialog box, navigate to the desired folder, select the desired XML file to be imported, and click Open.
4. In the Microsoft Office Excel information box, click OK to create a schema based on the XML data source.
5. In the Import Data dialog box, specify the location for the import.
   - Choose XML Table In Existing Worksheet and specify the location in the text box to place the import into an XML table in the active worksheet.
   - Choose Existing Worksheet and specify the location in the text box to place the import as flattened XML data.

A flattened XML table consists of a two-dimensional table that contains columns and rows. The column headings will be the XML tags and the rows below the column headings will contain the appropriate data. In cases where XML data is flattened, Excel will not infer a schema, and the XML map will not be available in the Source task pane.

- Or, choose New Worksheet to place the import in a new worksheet and place the data in the upper-left corner of the worksheet.

6. If necessary, in the Import Data dialog box, click Properties and set the import properties.

7. Click OK.

Procedure Reference: Export XML Data

To export XML data:

1. Open the file that contains the data that you want to export.

2. On the Developer tab, in the XML group, click Export.

3. In the Export XML dialog box, navigate to the folder where you want to store the exported XML file.

4. In the File Name text box, type a name for the file to be exported.

5. Click Export.

Managing XML Workbooks

The data in an XML-based workbook can be edited, deleted, cut, pasted, and sorted just like any other data in an Excel sheet.

Layout Limitations

When you want to import data into an XML-mapped worksheet, add new data to that worksheet, and then export all of the data, your XML map must appear as a contiguous list. This means that your mapped XML elements must appear as column headings in adjacent columns, and they cannot be separated from one another. To force XML elements to remain contiguous across adjacent cells, you can map them from left to right, across the column headings.

ACTIVITY 8-2
Importing and Exporting XML Data

Data Files:

Customer Data.xml

Before You Begin:

My New Customer Data.xlsx is open.

Scenario:

Your manager has sent you an XML file, Customer Data, that contains customer contact data. You decide to import the XML data into the My New Customer Data workbook, which uses the Schema2 schema. Finally, he needs to create an XML version of the file because he needs to send it to another department that doesn't use Excel. This new XML file needs to be named My Customer Data Update.

What You Do	How You Do It
1. **Re-create the map in the My New Customer Data workbook so that the XML elements are contiguous.**	a. In My New Customer Data.xlsx, **select the range A1:F2.**
	b. **Press Delete** to delete the existing mapping structure.
	c. **Display the XML Source task pane,** and using the Ctrl-click method, **select the Name, Street, State, and Country elements.**
	d. From the XML Source task pane, **drag the elements to cell A1.**
2. **Import data for the specified field from the Customer Data XML file into the My New Customer Data workbook.**	a. On the Developer tab, in the XML group, **click Import.**
	b. In the Import XML dialog box, **navigate to C:\084892Data\Structuring Workbooks with XML.**
	c. **Select Customer Data.xml and click Import.**

d. Notice that the XML data is imported into the mapped cells in the worksheet.

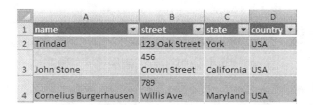

	A	B	C	D
1	name	street	state	country
2	Trindad	123 Oak Street	York	USA
3	John Stone	456 Crown Street	California	USA
4	Cornelius Burgerhausen	789 Willis Ave	Maryland	USA

3. **Export the data to a new XML file.**

    a. On the Developer tab, in the XML group, **click Export.**

    b. If necessary, in the Export XML dialog box, **navigate to the folder where you would like to store the exported file.**

    c. In the File Name text box, **type *My Customer Data Update* and click Export.**

    d. **Close the XML Source task pane.**

    e. **Save the Excel file as *My Customer Data Update.xlsx* and close it.**

Lesson 8 Follow-up

In this lesson, you structured workbooks with XML. Structuring workbooks with XML allows you to exchange data with other XML-compliant applications, thus enabling you to create data once and deliver it on multiple platforms in various visual layouts.

1. **How might you deploy XML-based workbooks in your organization?**

2. **What data do you have in existing documents that could be converted to an XML-based workbook?**

Follow-up

In this course, you automated some common tasks, applied advanced analysis techniques to more complex data sets, collaborated on worksheets with others, and shared Microsoft® Office Excel 2007 data with other applications. Advanced analysis techniques help you extract more value from your static data by summarizing and forecasting values that are not readily apparent in the static data. Using collaboration techniques helps you add value to your data and analysis of the data by allowing you to incorporate feedback of others into your data.

1. **Consider some Excel projects you are currently developing or are preparing to develop. How might these projects benefit from advanced analysis techniques?**

2. **How might you combine collaboration and advanced analysis techniques in your current or future projects?**

3. **How will you automate tasks in your Excel environment?**

What's Next?

This is the last course in the Microsoft® Office Excel® 2007 series.

Lesson Labs

Due to classroom setup constraints, some labs cannot be keyed in sequence immediately following their associated lesson. Your instructor will tell you whether your labs can be practiced immediately following the lesson or whether they require separate setup from the main lesson content.

Lesson 1 Lab 1

Customizing Your Workbook

Data Files:

Travel Expenses.xlsx

Before You Begin:

From C:\084892Data\Streamlining Workflow, open Travel Expenses.xlsx.

Scenario:

Currently, the Travel Expenses workbook contains three worksheets: April, May, and Totals. You know that in the future, most of the workbooks you will create will contain more than three worksheets, so you decide to increase the number of sheets in the workbook. Also, all the worksheets in the workbook should follow a specific format. The standards are:

- Draw attention to any monthly total that exceeds $2,000.00 by applying a light red fill to the corresponding cells.

- The value of the cells with numeric data should range only between 0 and 99999.

- The font size of the Totals row must be 14 points.

Instead of repeating the same task for all the sheets in the workbook, you need to find an easier way to automate the task. Later, you realize that the font size you choose is too large, but you don't want to redo the entire automation task to decrease it to 12 points.

1. Start recording a macro that formats the worksheets.

2. Apply light red fill conditional formatting to the Totals cells so that any monthly total that exceeds $2,000.00 is highlighted.

3. Force all of the cells that will take numerical data to only accept values in the range 0 to 99999.

4. Increase the font size of the Totals row to 14 pt.

5. Stop recording the macro.

6. Edit the macro to decrease the font size to 12 points.

7. Apply the macro to the remaining worksheet.

8. Change the default number of worksheets in a workbook to 10.

9. **Save and close the workbook.**

Lesson 2 Lab 1

Collaborating with Others Using Excel

Data Files:

Loan Amortization.xlsx, April May Travel.xlsx

Before You Begin:

Open the Loan Amortization.xlsx file from C:\084892Data\Collaborating with Others.

Open the April May Travel.xlsx file from C:\084892Data\Collaborating with Others.

Scenario:

You have two workbooks: Loan Amortization and April May Travel. You have completed work on the Loan Amortization workbook and want to distribute it to five of your colleagues, but you don't want them to alter any of the values or formulas in the file except the numerical values that represent the Principal Amount, Interest Rate, and Term in Months. You also want the changes they make to be highlighted so that you can later accept or reject them. All other values and formulas in the file must be protected.

You haven't finished development on the April May Travel workbook and you would like to get some feedback before you certify the file as production-ready. You decide to digitally sign the file so that the reviewer can verify your authenticity.

---

1. In Loan Amortization.xlsx, **protect the worksheet with a password of *password* so that the only cells that can be altered are the values for Principal Amount, Interest Rate, and Term in Months (use a range password of *P@ssw0rd*).**

2. **Turn the revision tracking on in the worksheet.**

3. **Digitally sign the April May Travel.xlsx workbook with your user name.**

4. **Close both files.**

Lesson 3 Lab 1

Auditing a Worksheet

Data Files:

Australian Division.xlsx

Setup:

Open the Australian Division.xlsx file from the C:\084892Data\Auditing Worksheets folder.

Scenario:

The Australian Division workbook contains sales data for four sales reps. However, one of the formulas in the worksheet doesn't seem to be working. You need to figure out why the yearly average cell isn't properly calculating the data and then fix the problem. Also, you would like to be able to view the yearly totals more easily without the detailed data for each quarter.

---

1. In Australian Division.xlsx, **trace precedents for each cell in the range B12:E12 and remove the arrows.**

---

2. **Trace the error in cell F12.**

---

3. **Watch the error in the Watch Window as you evaluate and fix it.**

---

4. **Create an outline for the 1st, 2nd, 3rd, and 4th quarters manually.**

---

5. **Save and close the file.**

Lesson 4 Lab 1

Analyzing Data in the Expense and Revenue Summary Workbook

Data Files:

Expense and Revenue Summary.xlsx

Before You Begin:

Open Expense and Revenue Summary.xlsx from C:\084892Data\Analyzing Data.

Scenario:

The management has given you the Expense and Revenue Summary workbook. They need to project expenses up to the year 2010. Additionally, they would like to know what would happen to:

- The 2003 profits if they had increased each revenue stream by 10 percent and the advertising budget by 20 percent.
- The cost of liability insurance if they had kept the 2004 expenses to $810,000.
- Each one of the 2005 revenue streams if the total profit was set to $250,000.

Finally, they need a way to summarize the product sales data quickly.

---

1. **Create a trendline on the Total Expenses Projection chart that extends out to the year 2010.**

---

2. For 2003, **create a scenario that increases each revenue stream by 10 percent and the advertising budget by 20 percent.**

---

3. For 2004, **use Goal Seek to project the cost of liability insurance if they had kept the 2004 expenses to $810,000.**

---

4. For 2005, **use Solver to project each one of the 2005 revenue streams if the total profits was set to $250,000.**

---

5. **Save and close the file.**

Lesson 5 Lab 1

Working with Multiple Excel Workbooks

Data Files:

Consolidate Sales Totals.xlsx, Consolidate Eco.xlsx, Consolidate Flanders.xlsx, Consolidate Smith.xlsx

Before You Begin:

From the C:\084892Data\Working with Multiple Workbooks folder, open Consolidate Sales.xlsx, Consolidate Eco.xlsx, Consolidate Flanders.xlsx, and Consolidate Smith.xlsx.

Scenario:

You are the manager of a small sales group in your company. You want to consolidate the data from three of your sales reps into a single worksheet so that you can see group totals at a glance. You would like to perform the following tasks:

- Create a workspace that incorporates the Consolidate Sales Totals workbook with the individual sales data located in the Consolidate Eco, Consolidate Flanders, and Consolidate Smith workbooks.

- Consolidate the data from the individual rep's files into the Consolidate Sales Totals workbook.

A month after sending the new file off to your manager, you decide to rename the Consolidate Sales Totals workbook to Consolidated Totals because the file will contain more information. You contact your manager and ask her to send the original file back to you so that you can edit the link in her file.

---

1. **Create a workspace from Consolidate Sales Totals.xlsx, Consolidate Eco.xlsx, Consolidate Flanders.xlsx, and Consolidate Smith.xlsx and name it *My Consolidated Workspace.xlw***

---

2. **Consolidate the Qty and Sales columns from each of the individual rep's files into the Qty and Sales columns of Consolidate Sales Totals.xlsx.**

---

3. **Open Consolidate Sales and Commissions.xlsx and link it to the Sales and Commissions total cells in Consolidate Sales Totals.xlsx.**

---

4. **Change the name of Consolidate Sales Totals.xlsx to *Consolidated Totals.xlsx***

---

5. **Edit the link in the file you sent to your manager so that it now points to Consolidated Totals.xlsx.**

---

6. **Save and close the files.**

Lesson 6 Lab 1

Importing and Exporting Sales Data

Data Files:

Circa US Sales.xlsx, Decker.txt

Before You Begin:

Open Circa US Sales.xlsx from C:\084892Data\Importing and Exporting Data.

Scenario:

You are consolidating the 2006 sales data for your manager. She needs you to:

- Make the contents of Circa US Sales.xlsx available in Microsoft Word.
- Store the contents of Decker.txt in an Excel file.
- Bold format the headings and adjust the width of the columns to fit the contents in the Decker workbook file in order to improve its visual appeal.

1. Export the contents of Circa US Sales.xlsx to Microsoft Word and then save the file.

2. Import the contents of Decker.txt into a new Excel file.

3. Format the file as necessary and save it.

Lesson 7 Lab 1

Publishing Excel Data to the Web

Data Files:

Math Web Page.xlsx

Before You Begin:

Open Math Web Page.xlsx from C:\084892Data\Using Excel with the Web.

Scenario:

The school you work for has decided to post all grades on its website. You have been asked to prepare your grading workbook for publishing on the web. The following tasks should be performed to ensure that the web page works as intended.

● Include the teacher's name and the class name on the web page title.

● Republish the web page every time it is saved.

● Preview the web page in the browser window.

---

1.   Publish the workbook as a web page.

---

2.   Change the title of the web page to *math – Mr. Harris*

---

3.   Change the file name to *My Math Web Page*

---

4.   Set options for autorepublishing the workbook every time it is saved.

---

5.   Preview the web page in a browser.

---

6.   Close all open files.

Lesson 8 Lab 1

Structuring the Property Listing Workbook Using XML

Data Files:

Property Listing Data.xml, Property Schema.xsd

Before You Begin:

Open a new Excel workbook.

Scenario:

Your manager has sent you two files: the Property Listing Data XML file and the Property Schema schema. She wants to view the contents of Property Listing Data in Excel. Additionally, she wants you to add the following two properties to the file, and then send her an updated XML file that she will forward to another group in the company:

- 7891 EFG Road is a Colonial with 2200 square feet of living space and is listed at $275,000.

- 5678 HIJ Place is a Dome with 1200 square feet of living space and is listed at $162,000.

You decide to create a new Excel workbook named Property Listing Info that is mapped to the Property Schema schema and that displays the data from the Property Listing Data XML file. You then update the Property Listing Info workbook with the new data and prepare it and also an updated version of the Property Listing Data XML file for mailing to your manager.

---

1. **Map the contents of Property Schema.xsd to the new workbook.**

---

2. **Import the contents of Property Listing Data.xml into the workbook.**

---

3. **Save the new workbook as *My Property Listing Info***

---

4. **Add the following data to the mapped region of the workbook:**
   - 7891 EFG Road is a Colonial with 2200 square feet of living space and is listed at $275,000.
   - 5678 HIJ Place is a Dome with 1200 square feet of living space and is listed at $162,000.

---

5. **Export the XML data by updating Property Listing Data.xml.**

Solutions

Lesson 4

Activity 4-1

2. **True or False? The trendline suggests that plate thicknesses of 13 or greater will result in 0 (zero) or fewer cracks.**

   ✓ True

   ___ False

Activity 7-3

1. **Which option allows you to determine the portions of a web page that are available for import?**

   a) A specific type of website.

   b) A specific format.

   c) The web administrator.

   ✓ d) The web query.

2. **True or False? The data inserted into a worksheet using a web query is updated automatically.**

   ✓ True

   ___ False

3. **Which option in the Get External Data group of the Data tab allows you to open the New Web Query dialog box to import data from the web to your Excel worksheet?**

   a) From Other Sources

   ✓ b) From Web

   c) Existing Connections

   d) From Text

4. **Which option in the New Web Query dialog box will allow you to adjust the way Excel imports data from the web?**

    a) Save Query

    b) Hide Icons / Show Icons

✓ c) Options

    d) Web page area

Glossary

cell dependent
A cell that contains a formula referring to other cells.

cell precedent
A cell reference in a formula that supplies data to the formula.

conditional formatting
A formatting technique which applies a specified format to a cell or range of cells based upon a set of predefined criteria.

data consolidation
A method of summarizing data from several ranges into a single range.

data validation
A validation technique which is used to restrict the value or type of data that can be given as input based on a specific set of criteria.

delimited text file
A TXT file that contains data fields separated by certain characters.

dependent workbook
A workbook that contains a link to another workbook.

digital certificate
An electronic file that contains unique information about a specific person.

digital signature
A content authentication tool that authenticates the sender and ensures the integrity of the digital document.

Error Checking
An option that is used to check for errors in a formula.

external reference
A reference to another workbook of the a defined name in another workbook.

file export
A method of transferring data that has been created in one application to a different application.

file import
A method of capturing data from one application for use in another application.

file publish
A method of publishing data that has been created in an application to a web page.

Invalid data
Any data in a cell that does not conform to the cell's data validation scheme.

IRM
(Information Rights Management) A service that permits users and administrators to define permissions to access presentations, documents, and workbooks.

macro
A task automation tool that executes a set of commands to automate frequently repeated steps.

Microsoft Office SharePoint Server 2007

A collaboration and content management server that is integrated with the Office 2007 suite.

module

A VBA code block containing one or more macros.

outline

A data organizing method in which a set of data is combined together to form a group.

revision tracking

A formatting tool used to track the person, date, and time of any revisions made to a workbook.

scenario

A set of input values that are substituted for the primary data in a worksheet.

shared workbook

A workbook that is set up and saved to allow multiple users on the same network to view, edit, and save the workbook at the same time.

Solver

A data analysis tool used to set the value stored in a single cell to a specified value by changing the value stored in multiple other cells.

source workbook

The workbook to which a formula refers.

tracer arrows

Graphic illustrations of the flow of data between cells that contain values and those that contain formulas.

trendline

A graphical representation of trends in a data series.

Visual Basic Editor

An add-in application you can use to load, view, and edit the VBA code for a macro.

Visual Basic for Applications (VBA)

The programming language used to create macros in Microsoft Office 2007 applications.

workspace

An Excel file that contains location, screen size, and screen position data about multiple workbooks.

XML map

An Excel component that maps the contents of an Excel workbook to an XML schema.

XML schema

An XML file that sets rules and defines the structure of other XML files of a particular type.

XML

A language that describes data by creating structured text files that are readable and easy to interpret.

Index